As the months wore
to survive, I was con
in the face of such a
Following one of his
asked his doctor to explain the science behind his miraculous
recovery. He just shook his head and said, **"It doesn't happen
that way. I can't explain it. Willie's explanation of divine
intervention is as good or better than anything I can offer."**
His story will help countless others. What a great read!

Mark Mintzer,
President, Global Patient Network

It has been my great privilege to know Willie Beeson personally
and to witness the remarkable transformation that his healing
has effected in his life. With his extensive medical evidence to
validate his testimony, he has deeply impacted my students each
semester when he comes into my classroom to tell his story.
His experience stands as a powerful demonstration that the
Kingdom power that Jesus wielded in his earthly ministry is still
active today. I rejoice that Willie's journey will now be available
to many others through this book, challenging and encouraging
them in their faith in God, and giving them a compelling window into the Kingdom that is yet to come.

Jonathan Lunde, Ph.D
Talbot School of Theology

It was William's miraculous story that began my own journey
into the supernatural. The details and documentation in his
book are utterly overwhelming. The Impossible Miracle will
amaze and inspire both skeptics and believers.

Joshua Tongol, apologetics speaker and youth minister,
Biola University B.A. in biblical studies

Willie's record is as true and dramatic as that of Paul's conversion on the road to Damascus. Through the crucible of hurt, hardship and healing, Willie Beeson changed from an ambitious, hard-driving businessman into a man seeking to know and please his heavenly Father. Willie shows us how when we put aside our pride, and seek God, we can find help.

Raymond D. Scott, Esq.

Yes! Jesus is alive and He heals today. Willie is a definite living proof that the Holy Spirit is still active in our midst. May anyone reading this book be encouraged, and find Jesus as the LORD and the Healer as Willie has received his miracle through his faith in Christ, and through the prayers of the believers.

John Park
Sr. Pastor of Father's House

It has been amazing to see the way God has changed the life of Willie Beeson. He is a walking (and jumping) testimony of God's power and love. Everywhere he goes, he tells his story to everyone he meets. May what you read inspire you the way it has inspired me. My faith has been strengthened. May you find God in brand news ways in the pages of this story!

Doug Green
Sr. Pastor, North Hills Church

You've read about miracles in the Book of Acts in the Middle East. Now you will learn about miracles happening today in the USA! William Beeson's story is a must read that will encourage you in your quest for Jesus' healing power in your life. I know Mr. Beeson-he is my good friend and brother in Christ-and I can testify to the genuineness of the miracle in his life. This book flies in the face of those who say that the day of miracles is over. God is still working in powerful ways!

Rev Simon & Anjana Gounder
Missionary with US Missions
Assemblies of God USA

This story is a testimony to the miraculous healing power of God and the necessity of persistence in prayer. I watched in horror as my brother descended into a living hell of excruciating pain, surgeries and drugs. I put my brother on prayer lists at churches all over Southern California. For eighteen months we called on the Father in heaven in the name of Jesus Christ to heal Willie. After the doctors started talking about amputating his left leg I grew desperate. We took Willie to the Father's House in Diamond Bar, Ca. I had heard that the Pastor John Park had the gift of healing. Willie was prayed for on Palm Sunday, 2005 by Pastors John and Michele Park. Nothing happened that day, but five weeks later God answered our prayers and Willie was TOTALLY HEALED!!! Be blessed as you read this amazing story.

Harry Beeson

Willie's testimony is a remarkable account of the love of our Father. His story will inspire you to believe that God is still a God of miracles and healing! His journey with God has expanded my own faith to see the realities of His love and the manifestation of His kingdom in not only other's lives but my own as well.

Ché Ahn
President of Harvest International Ministry
Senior Pastor, Harvest Rock Church

THE IMPOSSIBLE
MIRACLE

THE IMPOSSIBLE
MIRACLE

A TRUE ACCOUNT OF A MODERN
DAY MIRACLE

WILLIAM BEESON

TATE PUBLISHING & *Enterprises*

Published by Tate Publishing & Enterprises, LLC
127 E. Trade Center Terrace | Mustang, Oklahoma 73064 USA
1.888.361.9473 | www.tatepublishing.com

Tate Publishing is committed to excellence in the publishing industry. The company reflects the philosophy established by the founders, based on Psalm 68:11,
"The Lord gave the word and great was the company of those who published it."

Book design copyright © 2008 by Tate Publishing, LLC. All rights reserved.
Cover design by Jennifer L. Fisher
Interior design by Nathan Harmony
Author photo by Skip Rogers

Published in the United States of America

ISBN: 978-1-60462-546-2
1. Autobiography: Medical Tragedy
2. Self-Esteem: Courage
08.03.26

CONTENTS

ACKNOWLEDGEMENTS

I would like to thank all those important people in my recent life who have given their time and energy to make this book a reality. Without you I could have never made it through my amateur efforts at being a writer, let alone attempting to understand the many aspects of having a book published. I also would like to thank those who cared for me during my suffering.

First to Becky Czerwinski for the amazing way she easily transformed my wreckage of the English language into this beautiful work. Thanks go to Tate Publishing for guiding me through the uncharted waters of book publishing and editing. To each of the doctors and friends who gave permission to use their real names. To Dr. Quinones-Baldrich a heartfelt thank you for your kindness and help. To each of the many friends who contributed the quotes as only they could to this story, thank you.

To John and Michele Park, my eternal thanks for your faith, belief and prayers. To Dr. Che Ahn, thank you for the effect your faith has had on so many to open our eyes to healing prayer. To my brother Harry, for showing your unfailing love to me, to intercede for me at that last hour, to be prayed for one more time. Also, Harry your tireless efforts during those many months to seek prayer from the thousands of faithful worldwide. This is brotherly love, thank you! To those countless unseen faithful who prayed for me, thank you. To my close friends who showed their love by visiting me and encouraging me during those days. Thank you.

To my children Bonnie, John and Hannah for love and care during those difficult times, thank you. For my Mother who in her eighties witnessed this tragic suffering to her son, to the great day I surprised her with my healing, her one constant thought is and has always been to thank God for all we are given.

For my wife Darla, how does one thank a partner in marriage who truly shows through "better or worse, through sickness or health, through richer or poorer" the faith, the love, the endurance of seeing your spouse suffer, yet you held up to hold up our family. For your kind acts, your selflessness to me for the burden I placed on you during those dark days. For your graciousness to give me hope, to tell me "God loves you" even when I doubted it. To your keeping a strong face to me while you cried out in private, to staying with me when I became useless. For your faith, your own prayers to God to lighten this burden to give you strength during the deep valleys we faced. I want to tell you I love you and thank you. For without you I would not be here, nor have this story to share with the world.

To our God, our Creator who gave to me a new life, a second chance to live. This book is dedicated to You!

FOREWORD

At the sunset of a difficult life, a man found himself in a beautiful isolated beach. The setting sun cast a shadow of every imprint on the sand. Greeted by Him, the man was given an opportunity to review his journey. The man noted his life was reflected all along the shore, with highs and lows representing the success and sorrows of his life. There were footprints not yet washed by the waves from his birth up to where he was. "It is good to finally meet You", he said. "I have been with you all the way." As he heard this, he noticed that at times in his life there was one set of footprints, whereas in others there were two. The man soon realized that during the joyful moments of his life, two sets of footprints could be seen, highlighted by the setting sun. "Who was with me enjoying the times of success in my life?" "I was with you", He said. "Why did you leave me when things were difficult?" "I have always been with you. Those were the times when I carried you". *

The *Impossible Miracle* is the story of a man recognizing he is not alone in his journey. "We must open our eyes and heart to the truth." "I am like a child now in my trust of my Maker and His will for me. I am here to serve Him with my life that He alone has given to me to live in a path to serve Him." "God shows His wonders to us every day. We choose to ignore the beauty and the wonder of a marvelous Creator who desires us only to thank Him and honor Him." The author realizes these truths during his physical and spiritual healing. The grace received "is for your family and for those people who prayed for your remembrance of Me." As a physician, I have observed miracles every day. Most will credit science; some will credit man. At the end, the gift of faith shows that He is always with us.

Once, an eloquent and holy man told the story of a young girl. She prayed she would get a bicycle for Christmas. When asked by her priest why she wanted this bicycle, she explained that her mother was ill and thus she needed to go to the store to get what was necessary. The priest said, "Let us both pray that you get it." Three weeks after Christmas, the priest saw the girl in the playground and asked, "Did you get the bicycle?" "No" the girl answered. "I guess God did not hear our prayers," the priest stated. "Oh yes He did! He just said no". Prayer must be an unconditional surrender to God's will. The "Impossible Miracle" is a testament to this fact.

William J. Quinones-Baldrich MD
Professor of Surgery
UCLA Medical Center
Los Angeles, California

* Inspired by *Footprints in the Sand*, author unknown.

INTRODUCTION

How does one begin a story, albeit true, as incredible as this one? A story filled with horrible pain and suffering, depression, failed hopes, loss of control, and loss of a productive life. A story that shows the miraculous transformation of a man facing permanent disability to the restoration of his complete health even after being pronounced a hopeless case. A story where family and friends are waiting in a deathwatch for the final blow to fall on a once vibrant, strong-willed man.

For many this will be a story of wonder, a fantasy, for others at most disbelief. For some jaded cynics, this is just another anomaly of life that will someday have a scientific answer, but for now is somehow false. For all of you, I didn't write this to ask your opinion; I wrote this to show you, my family, and friends the real story of a miracle and to help those in pain, especially for those people who have given up all hope because of chronic suffering from a multitude of painful causes.

If my own story is inspiring and helps even one person on this planet to overcome their own suffering and to find the truth that God is alive and cares for each one of us, then this invest-ment of time and effort has a reward. I have prayed like some men or women for an end to my own suffering. An end to my suffering was also prayed for by thousands who didn't know me and by a few who did; those people know who they are.

They are the ones who believe in the power of prayer, as do millions around this world. Even medical professionals, work-ing in a purely scientific world, understand the mystery of prayer and miracle healings that defy all understanding. Why is this? What power can do this? How can a non-medical intervention cure cancer? Remove a blood clot? Restore a coma victim with damaged brain cells? I cannot answer these questions myself, but I know what happened to me and I have chosen to share it with you and with the world because I wish to proclaim the impossible miracle God has graced my family and me with: a second chance at life. Enjoy, cry, and rejoice with me, and with our Father in Heaven.

THE BEGINNING

Summer 2002

To begin this incredible narrative (and this being an especially powerful one), and enable you to know the whole story, some background information is required as it is in most stories. You need to know the characters and the message. So off we go into a journey that will defy your senses, tear your heart, and finally fill it with wonder.

As with all stories there is a beginning; mine began with a snap, or actually a fall. On a beautiful Father's Day in the summer of 2002, my family and I were enjoying a day of recreation and stress relief in the desert outside of Moreno Valley, California. On this day we were with friends riding in the dunes, sagebrush, and hills of the arid desert on all-terrain vehicles (ATVs). I had just recently purchased a matching pair of four-wheel-all-terrain-vehicles for my son and myself for our mutual enjoyment, believing this would bring us, as a family, some much-needed recreational time away from my insanely hectic contracting business.

As the day unfolded we found a suitable spot with one of my employees, Scott, who had knowledge of ATV's and the local area. My wife and I had asked if he and his family would take us to a nearby area and be with us in this new endeavor. We were all very excited, probably me most of all, as I was in much need of an outlet to relieve the pressure of my business affairs which were causing me great stress and worry over a business deal that had gone bad.

Our day was idyllic, and this family outing included my wife Darla, our oldest daughter Bonnie, our son John and our youngest daughter Hannah. We met our friend Scott, his wife Sue, and their son Kurt at their home, and we proceeded to the destination Scott was familiar with. For those whom are not seasoned ATV riders it is a good idea to have experienced riders along for an inaugural outing.

Although in my youth, in the military, I had ridden moto-cross on two-wheeled motorcycles, this world of four wheelers was altogether different, as we shall soon see. Scott located a spot near a grove of trees for shade, as it was quite warm, and with care and attention set up a day camp. Then we fired off these machines of fun and set off tentatively, Scott, Kurt, my son John, and myself. Soon we had conquered our fears of handling these machines; mine was a large displacement engine while John was on a small one appropriate for his age.

In short order my son had shown his knack for riding and was doing quite well. As the day progressed I became more fear-less in my riding as I recalled my youthful times and became accustomed to the handling characteristics of the ATV. I was soon mowing down the trails and paths and even going up small hills like in my youth, dreaming of Steve McQueen and the many Baja races he participated in with thousands of other off-road enthusiasts.

With my family stationed at the camp I periodically stopped by to take either my wife or daughters on a ride or let them handle the ATV. Our youngest, Hannah, was 5 years old and even more enthused than my son and couldn't wait for her turn on the cycle, of course with Dad on too, so we wouldn't crash. She was a full throttle kind of rider and I was compelled to provide throttle control to prevent us from running into trees or other riders. She was in a zone of her own fearlessness.

After everyone else had ridden, Bonnie finally asked if I would take her, as she was not comfortable riding by herself. Of course the manual does state one rider, but with a generous seat and after taking Hannah, it seemed like a normal and safe request. So after several hours of riding and being in the hot sun, and me not being in the best of shape, we set off to have a father and daughter moment, as she was soon to go to college. Moments like this had been few and far between. I was so happy she had come with us for this family event.

We proceeded to ride the trails and zoom through the desert roads feeling the exhilaration of the wind and the speed of the machine as we powered from place to place. She was holding onto me just as she had done as a little girl when I had taken her on bike rides or just carried her on my back while walking places. It was a wonderful time, just the two of us having a bonding moment once more before her next stage in life: college and career.

Finally, I slowed down as we came to a crossroad leading back to our camp and asked Bonnie, "Have you had enough?" I was tired, but she responded with, "No, let's go some more." So I viewed the landscape and looking ahead saw a road leading away and up, so I revved the cycle and away we sped to our new destination. As we climbed up this unfamiliar road, I realized we were going higher and higher and this concerned me, the road became narrower too. I thought of the danger of being on an unfamiliar hill, the first rule of cycling is to view all roads front and back, especially hills, before ascending.

However, here we were nearing the top, so I slowed down and came to a stop not realizing, due to my tired physical state of riding all day, that this was a mistake. As the ATV came to a stop just shy of the top the weight distribution of Bonnie on the back combined with downward gravity, immediately caused the quad to roll backwards. I mistakenly hit the brakes and yelled for her to jump as the quad made a seemingly timeless, slow arc over backwards. We landed and I cushioned the blow of the over 400 pound machine against my body. I yelled to Bonnie, "Are you okay?" She was smothered by me and wedged against sagebrush poised perfectly against the hill and she said, "I am fine, Dad."

I rolled the ATV away and stood up, lifting Bonnie and assessed our condition. She had a small burn on her upper arm from the hot exhaust and I was shaking with adrenaline from the moment, as I understood how narrowly we had just escaped from having broken bones or worse. We stood there and held each other and appreciated our good fortune. I then righted the ATV, looked over our position and realized we were standing on the precipice of a very tall hill. The fact that we had not tumbled several hundred feet down the hill was amazing!

I told Bonnie to begin walking down the path to the bottom of the hill. We were both shaken up, and I did not wish a repeat of my mistake of riding with two of us on the ATV. She began to walk while I righted the ATV and pushed it down the hill, actually down the ravine where it had come to rest. It was not a trail but a jumble of rocks and brush and uneven terrain. It was hot and I was very dirty, itching from the sand, dirt, and who knows what in my armor. Did I forget to mention that we all wore plastic body armor to protect us from falls?

Due to my uncomfortable state, I removed the armor and threw it up to Bonnie to carry. I kept my helmet on and continued to push the cycle down this ravine. As I progressed it became rockier and rougher. I viewed the way down and realized that just ahead was a small pathway back up to the road where Bonnie was walking. I yelled to her to wait, as I now sat on the ATV, started it, placed it in gear, released the clutch, and traversed to this short pathway.

As I hit this slope I was cutting diagonally across the face of the hill. Unfortunately, I hit soft windblown sand and the ATV began to roll sideways down the hill. I realized it was going, so I jumped up and pushed off the bike. It rolled away down to the rocks. I heard a loud female voice screaming, "No! Dad!" Then as my body was airborne, I attempted to rotate to see where I was going to land. This all happened in mere seconds as I arced down and rotated to the left, but not soon enough. My body struck a large rock on the lower left side of my left hip/back area.

As I hit and felt the concussion reverberate throughout my body I thought, *Oh, Oh, this is bad.* I then rolled over as a massive wave of pain and shock coursed through me. I was blacking out, and all I heard was Bonnie crying and screaming. I rolled over, crouched down, took some deep breaths, shook myself alert, and yelled, "I'm fine!"

I lifted myself up but began blacking out again; so I took a moment and stayed down to assess what was wrong. I took deep breaths and looked for the ATV. I found it several feet away still running while lying on its side. I moved slowly over to it, turned it off, and shut off the gas. Afterwards we found it had only suffered one torn fender and a slight burn from the exhaust on the other fender. What a tough machine Honda makes! If only bones were so pliable!

I turned to Bonnie and said, "Wait for me, and I will come to you." I did not want her to know the agony and pain I was in and that I knew I was severely hurt. As I took my first real step, I found that my left leg was paralyzed and I could not move it on its own. So I grabbed my pant leg and swung it up and grabbed a bush and slowly made my way up to Bonnie. She was crying and weeping for me. I made it to her, and as I stood up to show her all was well, I blacked out again.

I grabbed onto her to hold myself up, lowered my head to breathe and said, "Help me walk, we need to get back to camp."

She was in tears and saying, "I love you, Dad, I love you."

I said to her, "I love you too. Let's go, something is wrong with my leg."

We were approximately half a mile from our camp. That walk back was a timeless moment of pain thinking about how stupid I was and the close call with disaster. Not knowing what had happened to me, only speculating that I had possibly broken my left hip. My leg was numb and unable to function or hold my weight. As we slowly made our way to the camp area, I told Bonnie we must keep moving so I would not black out. We cautiously made our way with several stops as my body was trying to stop me and I fought to stay conscious.

Finally, after an interminable time, we hailed the camp; my wife came out and said, "What happened?"

I said, "Oh, we took a little fall, but I will be fine. Let me sit in the shade a minute. Um, where is Scott?" Darla led me to a chair and Bonnie described the accident, none of us knowing then the extent of my injury. When Scott arrived he immediately came to me and I told him quietly that this was a bad injury, to go get the ATV and return, and after that to go to the hospital, and to please not alert my family.

Scott went with his son and located the ATV but ended up leaving it there. They came back and loaded me in our truck. My wife followed and we set off for the hospital. Bonnie was with me, and I told her to keep me awake so she had to shake me whenever I started blacking out. I became incoherent and had slurred speech. Finally we arrived at Riverside County Trauma Center in Moreno Valley, a state-of-the-art medical emergency hospital built to handle accident victims from the multitude of injuries caused by incidents where people have fallen, suffered heatstroke, snake bites, and, of course, cycling and off-road accidents.

Once we arrived, I passed out and barely remembered anything from the emergency room, only that there were many doctors around as I passed in and out of consciousness. It was soon determined I had fractured three bones in my spine in the lumbar region. I also had received a concussion even though I was wearing my helmet. Evidently my head had struck the rock I had landed on after the initial impact to my hip.

Dazed as I was during this, I do remember snippets of that first evening. My wife was there, and once I saw Scott after he had gone back to get the ATV. He informed me it was intact and had sustained very little damage. I also remember my children being there and much discussion with the doctors as to what had happened. It was a very confusing time as everyone told the doctors something different, and since I was barely conscious and not talking they couldn't determine the full extent of my injury. Many tests were performed, and I was admitted to the hospital for observation.

This covers the first part of my story. Now we begin the rest of the journey leading to my miracle. The reason I was poised for my future ordeal was this ominous beginning. I had a fractured spine with massive soft tissue damage, yet the doctors determined after all the tests that it would be best for me to just let the fractured vertebrae heal on their own and surgery was not required. Two days later I was released, and even though it hurt to move, I went right back to work.

A week later I went for a post hospital check up with Dr. Edwards, who had been my family doctor for over ten years. He asked me how I had gotten to his office since I was alone. I replied, "I drove myself. I have been working since I was released." He reacted by throwing his, or actually my, chart up and said empathically, "With this severe an injury a slight bump from a pothole while driving could have paralyzed you! You must go home, stay off your feet twenty-three hours a day and lay flat on your back for the next six weeks in order for the bones to set and heal."

I was immediately shaken, as I had not understood any urgency from the hospital. They had led me to believe that the bones were encased in my back muscles and would be fine. Oh, the blessing of being ignorant as to our own body mechanics. This ignorance let me continue to physically abuse myself. So, following my doctor's orders, I returned home, contacted my staff and partners and informed them I would be conducting business from my home for the next six weeks. And I did.

What an amazing occurrence! I had suffered a stunningly close call to permanent disability, had walked out of the hospital and avoided surgery only to go blindly back to work (the concussion did linger). Then I heard from Dr. Edwards the true seriousness of my injury! I was blind to this as I was mired in my business affairs and the ongoing struggle to build the contracting company, which I had bought into just three years before.

My partner started this company three years before that. He and I had worked together previously at another company. He left to start up this business. After a year he had also purchased a small service shop and was buried in the merging of this company, jobs, and staff with his original business. We met during a negotiation I was making to go into business myself in 1999. I had found a small business I desired to buy and go into contracting too, and I asked for his help to service some of these accounts. He didn't know I was intent on buying the company, but as time went on he found out. As things go, my deal fell through, but he seized the opportunity of my unhappiness at my current employment to make me an offer.

So in the summer of 1999, I joined my partner and within

days sold my first commercial job contract, and we never looked back. The company zoomed from a three-person affair to within a year employing over twenty people and jobs, jobs, jobs. We outstripped our cash so many times it was insane. Our bottom end was bottomless as we grew at triple pace month after month. If it hadn't been for my partner's in-laws, seasoned self-made entrepreneurs with ready cash to fund us, we would have hit the wall within months.

By 2002 we were riding a wave of success and growth that to us was seemingly unparalleled. Even though we made mistakes, we seemed to be able to weather the storms of a too fast growing business coupled with all the growth pains of non-stop action. The biggest loser being my relationship with my family as I toiled incessantly for this ever-consuming business that every day needed more and more hours and six and seven days a week to handle the ongoing sales, operations, accounting, production, money needs, customer relations, employee relations, and all the other aspects of a budding venture. An all-devouring beast I had created as part of the American Dream of business entrepreneurship. However, it was destroying my marriage and making me one unhappy and stressed fellow. Of course there were good moments, and I had always dreamed of achieving the kind of security from all my hard work and sacrifices that would one day allow me to enjoy the fruits of my labors.

So it was actually with some relief, in spite of the pain, to have a few weeks of downtime to spend with my family and be home for the first summer ever instead of being in the middle of my typically busiest season. Of course I was doing what the doctor ordered and staying flat on my back to allow healing. I conducted my business affairs from my couch and spent endless hours on the telephone. But it still was a pleasant time to be there with my family during the summer of 2002.

August came and with it the peak of our business. Now I was

ready to return to work and I did. My bones had healed perfectly and the orthopedic doctor felt everything was fine. Even though I said I was still in great pain and it was hard to bend, he said nothing was wrong. I think this meeting lasted one minute. He was in a hurry. My wife and I were perplexed as to why I was still in pain. But, oh well, he said I could go back to work and eagerly I did just that.

What an ominous return it was. A bare two months away from the company, and it was a shambles of conflict. Upon my return it was like the Western Front of WWI had erupted full scale. Clients were ready to fire us, employees were ready to quit, major projects were faltering, and we had no cash; not a pretty sight to return to.

My first acts were to correct the client issues and turn that around; I hired a consulting company to help us to unify our people in our activities. Very expensive, but very necessary! Got more cash to operate (we borrowed more from partner's in-laws) then I began to right the faltering jobs and get more sales. Unfortunately the bottom fell out; this happened because we had grown so quickly and outpaced our cash. During this time my accountant had missed many payments to everyone, including workers' compensation, health insurance, critical vendors, and even the IRS.

October 2002

I was faced with having to let my accountant go. It really tore me up, as I knew my accountant tried her best. It was just that our system of accounting was flawed from day one. Even with a very painful back I began working twenty hours a day, six and seven days a week, as the business manager, production manager, salesman, and accountant to deal with these overwhelming issues.

It was catastrophic in proportion. Our insurance had lapsed

for non-payment, our workers' compensation was close to cancellation, the IRS conducted an audit, and also the State of California. Projects were behind and staff was confused. Yet, through it all I persevered and with the new cash infusion we managed, and with getting jobs righted and payments in, we survived the most awful time of the young company's life.

Late 2002

However, it was personally devastating and took a heavy toll on my health. I was barely able to move as my back was in constant agony. I took pills and pills and couldn't get relief. I had finally gone to a new orthopedic doctor after asking Dr. Edwards for help. This new doctor, Dr. Hanlon, determined that I had soft tissue damage to the left hip/back area and began a series of cortisone shots, Vicodin pills, and muscle relaxants.

Early 2003

I was not progressing. Dr. Hanlon sent me in for physical therapy, which I began in February. This was the solution! Beginning with these basic exercises and modalities it forced me to get away from the office and begin to take care of myself. I was a wreck, bloated to over 250 pounds. Not able to move or bend, any activity cost me hours of bed rest if I could get it. With an auspicious beginning under Dr. Hanlon's care, my pathway to restoring my health began.

Simultaneously the business was stabilizing with new sales, a new in-house accountant, and my slow process to recover my body. As these months ticked by I was able to restore my health due primarily to taking the time to invest in my family and myself. This was crucial to getting well. Why is it that our society demands such a price from us? Or is it simply the affliction of being a workaholic? Was I such a person who couldn't control my own life and allowed all these monsters of attachment to run me into the ground and nearly destroy me? I was simply trying to get ahead, and it seemed the further I went, the deeper I got!

Thankfully my own doctor and my wife rescued me by insisting that I take the time to recover. Only I was going at this insane pace and driving myself into a premature grave. So I began my own restoration slowly, painfully easing away from high blood pressure/hypertension and worry to doing for the first time in years something for me to help me get my health back.

During these pivotal months I drew away a little from the daily ongoing affairs of the business, delegated more and more to the accountant, my partners, and staff. I took the time to embrace the physical therapy sessions and began to feel my body heal. After four months I was finished with my sessions and returned to see Dr. Hanlon. He was pleased. However, I wasn't. I could still not bend well and felt like there was more to do. So I inquired of Dr. Hanlon, if it would be okay for me to hire a personal trainer and do a supervised exercise program that he would approve. He responded very positively, and so I soon joined a fitness club and hired a trainer, a suitable young man named Rick. He had some medical background as an EMT and was an experienced personal trainer. We went over my history, and then I revisited Dr. Hanlon for his approval and so we began the next phase of the journey.

Without too in-depth a history of this, Rick and I began a simple program of stretches to loosen the impacted muscles (soft tissue) and to restore the once pliable muscles that were stiff from that year-old impact with the rock. Within weeks I was doing much better. In fact Rick commented for a back patient I was making remarkable progress. Indeed by the time of my next follow up with Dr. Hanlon, I was able to not only bend at the waist, I could touch my toes, and even do terrific leg splits!

Dr. Hanlon even commented that I looked great (I had lost

twenty pounds) and it was in his observation, a remarkable turn-around considering the short time since this started (three months). So he said, "Continue this and stay away from motorcycles. Come see me only if you need to—you are doing fine. Keep it up."

So I left him and was elated, to say the least, as it had now been just over a year from the accident, and now my life was good. I was getting very healthy and fit. I continued my training with Rick with the good news, and so we began in earnest to improve my condition and lose more fat and build muscle, all the while strengthening my back carefully. During these fun-filled weeks it was good to continue doing what I needed to improve my health and achieve fitness after going through what I thought was the worst experience I had ever had.

Our family life was stable again. Bonnie was in college, Darla was working and happy, John and Hannah were doing well in elementary school. My business—well, it was improving, and for the most part, I was handling the pressure better and letting things take their own course and just for once enjoying the moment. I was getting very fit; indeed I was down 40 pounds from my peak of 250 pounds early in the year. I was adding muscle and doing very well activity-wise. Going back to my passion of ice skating and playing with the kids and doing work around the house, etc. Life wasn't perfect; we had our worries, the ongoing worry of the business and all, but things were better.

THE SPINE

For everyone who has ever had back pain, it is without a doubt the most irritating and frustrating chronic aspect of trouble to our health. It is one of the most costly economic health issues facing mankind today. Even with the best medical care more time is lost through spinal injuries, more workers' compensation dollars spent, more in health cost to this most often misunderstood, simple, yet highly complex, precise structure to our body.

What is the spine? First off, I am not a medical person, and if I have stated something improperly, blame my ignorance as a non-medically trained person. I am just a layman, although a somewhat knowledgeable person, having undergone some of the most extensive surgeries available for my spinal injuries.

The spine is a structure made up of bones and soft tissue. The bones are a functional arrangement of stacked sections, arranged vertically with precisely made protrusions to balance one atop another, kind of like stacking cupcakes with only a bit more engineering.

You may also liken this to a modern multistory building

with the floors rising from the foundation (sacrum) vertically to the lumbar section (the section of greatest loading) to the thoracic section (mid back/ribcage) to the cervical section (neck and head) culminating in the skull. This comprises the spinal column bone elements.

Each individual element is called vertebra, which are wonderfully designed bone structures that provide the structural integrity to our spine as well as housing our spinal cord, the superhighway that transmits our electrical signals from each tissue, cell, and component of our body to our brain. The vertebra is formed with an interconnecting channel surrounded by bone to protect the spinal cord. This system has been precisely created to allow for movement without the slightest impact to this precious cord.

Supporting each vertebra or bone element is a gel-filled fibrous membrane called the nucleus populous, which is contained within another fibrous membrane encasing the nucleus. This is called the annulus populous. This cushioning system is called the intervertebral disk system. It provides the spinal column with flexibility and with shock absorption from pressures exerted upon the spine in movement and loading.

Holding all this structure together is a system of bands called ligaments. These begin at the skull and encase the entire spine in a multi-striated fashion sweeping down to the sacrum section. These tight bands attach at the boney protrusions stated earlier called the spineous processes. This structural design maintains an intact skeletal spinal column that can bend in lateral, flexion, and extension directions and not fall apart. Envision a cable suspension bridge that has the tightly wound steel cables that hold the sections of the bridge aloft without posts or pillars sunk into the earth to support the far-sweeping spans.

To allow us to move this beautifully designed system, we have an intricate system of heavy and light layered specifically tailored muscles or more fibrous bands that respond to our brain's signals moving at the speed of electricity throughout the spinal cord's nervous system to either voluntarily or involuntarily conduct specific actions to rotate or move our spine. These muscles, approximately one hundred and forty, provide through another intricate connection system of tendons, inserting at the many points in the spinal system. This allows our many other skeletal bones a unifying structure that we can articulate freely within the range of motion granted by this miraculously designed body we have.

Of course we typically know not of this as we spend each day in absorbed activities, and we assume our magnificent bodies are performing and functioning properly. All we have to do is provide fuel and fluid to keep this machine, if you will, going literally non-stop for hours, until our internal systems relate to our brain it is time for a rest to allow other important processes, i.e. our internal organs, which perform a seemingly inexhaustible series of functions and tasks on a microbiological level, to perform their important functions to maintain this completely beautifully designed technological wonder.

Obviously a doctor could explain far more precisely the many involved systems of the human body than I have here. I have tried to express in a very brief method the essence of the miracle of the spine and to give the reader a minimal overview for the purpose of appreciating this marvelous system we take for granted, that we abuse daily and curse it as it responds in pain signals generated by one or more of the systems that has become weakened or has sustained an injury or has a systemic problem.

As in my ATV accident, the muscles impacted were so injured they had many spasms to the point of being seized, which is a natural reaction of the body to prevent further damage. This condition can last for days and be very debilitating. Regardless of the level of pain, if it is soft tissue, meaning inflamed muscle tissue or an inflamed nerve, and then treatment through rest, ice, heat and non-use is prescribed to start. If you seek care from a doctor, especially an orthopedic doctor, you may be prescribed anti-inflammatory medications or even muscle relaxants with some pain management combination.

Typically for soft tissue injury the body will heal itself if, and only if, we cease the offending activity and allow time, approximately two weeks, to heal. Certainly in most cases a few days rest will lead to significant improvement. For those situations that are more severe, and when we are in constant pain, our only desire is for relief. Then we seek medical attention and as required may then go ahead with specialists trained in the complex field of back care.

This amazing field is coupled with the incredible ability of modern medical technology to intervene using the most sophisticated man-made inventions and equipment to attempt mind-boggling solutions to our pain. From using non-invasive treatments, i.e. massage, braces, rest, medications, or physical therapy; to invasive treatment using bits of metal or bits of bone and some fastening hardware to create a solid unit where there was once a completely non-functioning damaged vertebrae or diseased disk and restore; to the patient, a higher level of life-style with less dependency on pain-killing drugs. For many of us this is the only hope.

I have, through my own experiences, traversed all of these kinds of treatments. I will now begin to tell the tale of hope and restoration through placing my faith and belief in God, and listening with my heart to His grace, that through the healing power of my Lord and Savior Jesus Christ, I was healed and given a new life to live, to share and to proclaim this awesome and impossible miracle that defies all medical science.

THE MACHINE

September 2003

After months of personal training with Rick and achieving a certain level of success, I went ice-skating. It was one of the passions of my youth that I continued to enjoy as an adult with my family and friends whenever we could go. In September of 2003, I finally went ice-skating for the first time since my ATV accident and recovery.

I may have been over enthusiastic and skated too much because my lower left back began to throb and became painful. This was my first flare up of the back since I started training with Rick in June. Over the next few weeks it seesawed back and forth, with Rick stopping training to give me massages to help with the sore tissue, until one Saturday late in October it was bad. In fact, Rick, at our early morning Saturday session, noticed my favoring this and checked my back and wouldn't allow me to exercise or have a massage and said go have it checked by a doctor.

October 2003

So I took his instruction and went to my chiropractor, whose office was unfortunately closed. So I suffered through the weekend only doing light stretches until that coming Monday. Coincidently my wife had an appointment with a different chiropractor very close to our home and who took our insurance, a real plus. Consequently, I decided to join her on her consultation and listened to the chiropractor explain his methods. He was quite thorough.

I inquired as to getting treated and we set an appointment for my consultation a day later. At that time we went over my history. He then performed the modalities and an adjustment, a method of grabbing your arm and leg and cracking your back with a loud snap. I wasn't sure if I was okay or not, but he seemed to think it had gone well.

After a few of these sessions over two weeks, my sacrum joint (what the doctor called it) was tight again. Indeed I felt better and was able to continue training with Rick. All was well.

The doctor informed me of a machine that he owned. From reviewing my condition, he suggested that using it would help strengthen my upper back muscles that were weak from the ATV accident. He had decided this from his examination of me and from my reaction to the treatment. I thought I was doing well; my journal sure reflected that.

Later I discussed this with Rick and asked if he would join me in a day or two to look over the machine the chiropractor had shown me. When he did, Rick and the doctor talked and discussed it. Meanwhile I warmed up and was given the initial test. That was all that was done on that day in early November. The doctor had warned Rick and me about working out after using this machine, especially the back, on the days I used the machine.

After we left Rick expressed his opinion that this machine was not needed because we were doing fine. I listened to him and assured him I would talk to the doctor about his concern. A couple of days later, at my first exercise session, I met with the doctor and expressed Rick's concerns.

He replied that this was advanced technology, it was safe, and extensively tested. No one had ever been hurt on it. I considered what he said and believed that he had told me the truth. As a result, we began exercises on the machine that the computer determined were what I needed. This determination was for only a nominal six sessions due to the good health my back showed and my strength from training with Rick, *hmmm*.

November 2003

Instead of detailing each day or session, let it be said we did the six sessions, and I kept progressing up in the number of repetitions and weight to the maximum allowed. By the end of November, I was easily performing the maximum of thirty reps using a startling weight resistance of over two hundred pounds. I continued my training with Rick in between these sessions and with his input on supplements and vitamins. I was steadily gaining muscle mass and getting very strong. In fact I was looking trim, yet very muscular.

Thanksgiving came, and we broke for the family holiday. We traveled to Las Vegas to visit my wife's family who resided there. I recorded all my activities in my workout journal and my looking forward to the last session/test on the lumbar machine on Monday the 1st of December. We came home on Sunday, and I unloaded our motor home and cleaned it. Then I went to the club to do my cardio workout and stretching, and to use the spa to relax before going back to work on Monday.

I really felt great; I was looking forward to seeing the results from the upcoming final test on the lumbar machine. This was a very different type of rehabilitation therapy from any I had ever experienced, and it was going well. With the last test ahead, I would now be released. I was looking forward to my renewed health and ongoing training with Rick. Life was good.

The first ominous sign was when I left the chiropractor's office on the Wednesday before Thanksgiving. They had switched my final appointment for the test from Monday December 1st to the morning rather than my normal after-work routine. This was going to be with a new doctor, not the trainer who had performed my sessions.

December 1, 2003

Everything, it seemed that morning of December 1st, went normally. I met with the new doctor who asked me to warm up as always and do my pre-machine exercises. I did them and she asked me how I felt. I said fine. She asked me to get into the machine and set up my test, which I performed. She said I had done a most excellent test. Then, leaving me strapped in the machine (you need help to get out), she asked me if I desired to work out. I said, "Here or on the floor?"

She replied, "On the machine."

I asked her why, because the chiropractor and the other trainer on the machine had insisted that after using the machine for exercise or testing that you were not to work the back, as it is so stressful. She said that I was strong and had nothing to worry about. I asked why again.

She asked, "Are you afraid?"

I said, "No, I am not afraid, but I do not wish to get hurt."

She then said, "Everything will be fine, other people do this."

I said, "Well, if you assure me that this is fine and I will not get hurt, then I will put my trust in you."

She said, "You have nothing to fear, you completed a good test and you are strong."

When using this machine, you always start in the fully flexed position. In my condition at that time I could sit and put my chest to my knees. So here I was fully flexed and I began this new exercise, just a mere minute after performing the strenuous test, not thinking my muscles were exhausted. So I started up and reached the top and began to come down.

The new doctor told to me to slow down, that I was going too fast. I then came down and counted with her coming up. The weight was heavier now. I made it up to the top and came down to the flexed position.

As I began to come up from the fully flexed position a loud snap sounded in my ears, and I felt like my left hip socket had popped out of the joint and the bone pulled away. Then with great force the tendon and ligaments snapped back into place. Subsequently, a most excruciating pain blasted through my left side, leg, and back. I screamed to her to stop the machine and get me off! She was screaming that it was my fault that I was going too fast!

My leg felt like it had been electrocuted with thousands of volts of electricity (yes, I have had high voltage shocks in my career). This was insanely intense. I had to flex all the way forward to get relief from this pain and still it felt like burning fire was scorching my leg all throughout the muscles and tissue. The pain was so white-hot intense I was quickly passing out and yelled to her again to get me off the machine!

She was screaming. Someone came and the two of them un-strapped me and quickly pulled me off the machine. They quickly carried me, half-crouched over from the pain, to a room close by and closed the door. The chiropractor came in and asked what had happened. She was hysterical. I was hunched over in great pain and going into extreme shock!

The doctor looked me over and then told her to give me a heat and ultrasound treatment. He asked if I could stand; I said no. He left and she went to get the heating pads and the ultrasound equipment. She returned and began to harangue me about how it was entirely my fault. I told her this was not the time to blame, that I needed help. She then put the heat pads on me and began to apply the ultrasound treatment. Once completed, the doctor came back and asked how I was. I responded that I was still in great pain and felt like the muscles in my left leg had been shredded.

He instructed her and someone else to lift me up and placed me on a table. Then he gave me one of his trademark adjustments, cracking me in the lower back. I was in immediate shock and great agony from this and was becoming incoherent. He said that I was okay to go home, to put heat on my leg, and come back in a few days. He wrapped a bandage on my upper thigh under my pants.

I stumbled to the hallway; my left leg was shooting in pain. I loosened my pants and removed the bandage. I tried to stand up and as a consequence howled from the pain in my leg and back. Right then my trainer came up and asked what had happened; I told him. He said, "We need to get you an ambulance!" I said, "Just help me stand." He held me and we slowly made it to the hallway counter and to the secretary. He told her to call 911. She shook her head while staring at me.

I kept breathing laboriously and was holding onto him. The secretary demanded payment, so I gave her some money. Then I asked him to help me to my truck outside. He kept saying he would take me to the hospital. I said no, just get me in my truck. I knew I had Vicodin at home and thought it would help.

He was so concerned; he was a decent caring person. He lifted me like a baby into my truck and again said he would go get an ambulance from across the way. I said no. I started my truck and said good bye and drove away with my head laying on the window, my body bent over in a most peculiar way trying to help with the immense pain I was suffering. On the way home

I called Rick and Darla and said I was hurt and to come get me (we lived a mile or less away). When I made it home I fell out of the truck onto the lawn. They came and lifted me into the car and drove me to the hospital emergency room.

WHO I AM

———•─◦─•———

Are you wondering if there is something special about me? That something I did "earned" me a miracle? Well, there isn't. My life has been no different than all of yours.

I was born in 1957 in Arcadia, California, the last child of my parents Harry C. Beeson and Gwenyth M. Beeson. I have two sisters and one brother. My parents had moved from Santa Monica, California in 1955 to Covina because my oldest sister Judy and brother Harry had contracted polio and the doctors had advised my parents they needed to move to a warmer climate for the health of Judy and Harry.

So they sold their small home in Santa Monica and, finding a suitable new housing development in the urban town of Covina, moved to their new home and to improved health for my siblings. The doctors were right, and soon my sister and brother were recovered from the polio attack and were able to regain the full use of their legs, and life became good again.

In 1956 my mother gave birth to my sister Rebecca in April and I came along in October of 1957. Life in Covina in my family was stable, fun, and of course with older siblings, Judy was thirteen and Harry seven when I was born, it was a rollicking place, full of activity and always a warm, safe place to be. With plenty of people coming and going and of course having a cool brother that I could tag along and bother was the most fun.

It was the best time a young boy could grow up in the late fifties and the early sixties when inflation was low, low interest rates and debt non-existent. No wars or major issues, just a good time to be alive and enjoy the early years of life with lots to do and fun Sunday rides in a big Buick to the far-off locales like Corona or Los Angeles.

Covina was famous for orange groves then, and as I reached the ripe age of five or so, it was fun to walk to the end of the street we lived on and be in a grove of orange trees. The streets were not all paved yet and didn't have curbs so it was all so fresh and lively. My Dad delivered milk, a really cool job then, and we would wait for him to come by in the afternoons with the big truck and open the door and let us have a container of chocolate milk or at times a frozen ice cream.

Also cool were the days the Helms truck came by and we had to be sure the sign was up in the window so he would stop and we would zoom out the door. He would open that back door and pull out that drawer lined and oozing with sugar and we could pick one sugary donut for a nickel I think, then we would race back to the porch and just hang out with another well-deserved treat.

Soon my sister Judy moved out as she went to college or to work. All I knew was my sister was leaving and it was the end of the world, as I knew it. She was so cool; she would bring her friends over, listen to records, smoke cigarettes (I wasn't supposed to tell), and have me clean up the house for them. I loved it all, and I loved Judy; she was so wonderful and sweet.

Then there was Harry, my brother. Well, you could say we

didn't see eye-to-eye. He had so many neat things in his room, and I just couldn't stay out of there. I mean I just had to open his drawers and closet and pull out his boats, or scout stuff, or models, and run around with them. Only for some reason he would always find out I did it. It was the end of the world when I had to start kindergarten and couldn't sneak in his room when he was at school.

Of course there was also Becky (Rebecca), my archrival for everything. Since she was a year and a half older, and a girl, my life was doomed. She kept a short leash on me and would advise Dad of my daily activities. This was a real snafu that required total planning on my part to escape her ever-watchful eyes. So I learned to open the screen door and front door very quietly and run like the wind to the garage before she knew I was out of the house and on to some new adventure.

The garage was a land of mystery and filled with treasures and jewels to a very inquisitive boy who needed to explore each thing without the prying eyes of a sister or for that matter, Mom or Dad. It was great when I could find time to get away to that place of dust and oil and weird bottles and strange tools and old military stuff and car parts and just dream away the days.

Life was a fun time and it is a wonder to recall those times day after day before the world erupted into worry and concern over Dad losing his job, Vietnam, school, homework, Uncle Pablo dying, Harry off to college, Grandma Rees dying, me in high school, considering what to study for a career, girls, more homework, getting a part-time job, learning to drive a car, etc. The oil embargoes, Nixon resigning, the rock and roll times, and let it live. Getting ready for graduation. Going in the military. Getting shipped to Japan. Really growing up. Lonely times, yet the best of times, seeing a beautiful country and meeting exotic people and cultures.

More military business to learn, shipping out to Italy for tour number two. I was learning Italian and really traveling to places no one in my family had seen. The Adriatic Ocean, Brindisi, Bari, white beaches, clear blue azure waters, the food! I got to housesit off base and had fun parties. I received a cool military honor and medal.

I finally came home and found out that the world was safer overseas than on the streets of Covina and Los Angeles. It was hard to adjust, Dad wanted me to cut my hair and get a job. I wanted to enjoy life some so I traveled around and soon got a job in air conditioning. Work, work, work. I lived at home, spent time with family and friends, got a new job with a family friend's uncle working at a small refrigeration business.

Dating, more dating, working, and going to hang out with friends. Everyone was still the same except me; I had been changed by my world travels and different languages; military speak, you know. In January I saw Darla, my long-time friend from high school. We went out, and then six months later we were married. Wow. It's 1982.

A new job, a good one, we bought a house using my VA bill. Life was wonderful and busy. 1984, our daughter Bonnie was born on September 11th. More changes, my Dad and Mom retired. I changed jobs. In 1986 we moved to Sacramento, which was a really big change!

On and on, a business start up, stress and hard times, bought another house. I finally got out of business, and landed a good job. A nice summer spent traveling. I actually had time to be with Darla and Bonnie. I broke my leg, recovered and went into sales. A whole new twist on my career, then a transfer to Santa Rosa, California. I loved it there, but it was not good on my relationship with Darla, which became strained. So I left that job and got on with a local company that was much better.

Dad had surgery, 1992. I took a leave of absence and decided it was time to move back to Covina. It was tough on Darla, since she had adjusted to Santa Rosa. But my folks needed me, and it was heartfelt. We moved and I got a new job as a manager of a company. It was good. We bought another house, a nice one in Brea, Orange County. Life was stable and good, life with Mom and Dad was good too. It was a renewing time.

Oops, stork arrived again, this time a boy, John born July 17, 1995. A cool dude. What a major change, Bonnie was eleven, moving up and on, and we are starting over. Oh, oh, another stork brought us Hannah, a girl, born August 7, 1996. She was born eight days after my Dad had passed on from pancreatic failure. It was a tough go, and a rough time for Mom and all of us. He was a solid, tough, yet heart-of-gold guy. I miss him a bunch. Hannah, our precious gift from God, helped offset this loss.

We moved Mom and sold the house. We kept busy with lots of kids' things: parties, showers, birthdays, you name it. There was always lots of work to do. I worked on the house, the yard, the cars, the kids, and, of course, my job. This was a really fun time that was full of happenings. Then I got itchy at work, as things weren't going well. It was 1999 and I decided to leave and go into business. Darla was not pleased. The kids were young and this put added pressure on her. But I was really unhappy. Boy, what a mistake, I realized later. But God is always faithful and even when we are full of pride and self, He is waiting to pick us back up.

I had now come to the point of our life where we had magnified stress and then my accidents occurred: first the ATV, then the machine. There was a short respite for a few months after the first accident as we recovered. Then, with the second accident, the sky truly fell and with it all our hopes. I thank God that He was ever faithful and unfailing in His love for us. For without it, my family would never have made it through the upcoming hell.

FROM A DISASTER TO
A CATASTROPHE

December 1, 2003, continued

With Rick and Darla, we arrived at the local hospital in Brea, and they rushed me into the emergency room in the most excruciating pain I had ever experienced in my life. I could not stand straight. I was bent over with no inclination to move, as the slightest movement caused shearing pain levels in my back and leg.

With the ER tech and Rick, I am lifted to a gurney and taken into the ER room. As they begin the questions as to what happened, I am not too patient and plead for a morphine shot to stop the pain. They responded that I must lie down so they could get my vitals. In fact, one tech tells me, without my cooperation, they cannot help me. This led me to explode in verbal rage that I will leave and go to another hospital where I could receive proper treatment.

Darla and Rick were further incensed over this, and they got the ER doctor to see me and without ado, I got a shot. Then another one since the first does nothing. The doctor was very concerned over my pain level and advised me to try and relax. I told him I couldn't straighten out; if I did the pain would ramp up tremendously. He was compassionate and said I could stay right there bent over, that hopefully the shots would soon take effect.

I was incredibly scared, sweating, and hyperventilating; the pain was so blinding even with the morphine shots. The doctor ordered an X-ray of my lower back/pelvis. They wheeled me to the radiologist and as I could not lay flat for the test, the radiologist had the nurse come and gave me another morphine shot. She did. Then the radiologist asked if I could lay back and allow the X-ray to be taken. I replied, "I will try, but no promises as the pain is so bad."

I laid back and screamed as I tried to straighten out, the pain shooting through my body was so white-hot intense and I felt like I would pass out. The nurse and radiologist came to me and said this will only take a few seconds. Could I manage? So I took a sharp breath, and with them right there, I screamed as I lay back flat and the radiologist took the X-ray. I surged up as my heart raced to maximum heartbeats and screamed with the most intense blinding pain. I began to vomit my guts on the table.

The nurse immediately gave me another morphine shot and in seconds I passed out. Several hours later I came to and the ER doctor came to tell me they could do nothing for me; I needed to see my orthopedic doctor. He had the appointment set already, and then he released me to go home. They gave me another morphine shot for the ride home since I was not able to move from that bent position. Now I was thoroughly drugged and still in pain. I was so groggy it was hard to remember the next couple of days.

The next day I was at home resting and taking loads of Vicodin every 2 to 3 hours. I had shooting pains through the leg, and I couldn't walk. A neighbor brought over a set of crutches. This was a big help. I was simply wiped out and in such horrible pain. What has happened I asked? Was this a ripped muscle? I was so confused and needed help. I was having trouble going to the bathroom, nothing was working right, and it was impossible to move.

Journal Entries

December 3, 2003

Darla took me to see Dr. Hanlon, my orthopedist. Thank God for those crutches as I hobbled into the office. Dr. Hanlon examined me and ordered an MRI X-ray. He voiced his opinion that I had ruptured a lumbar disk and the MRI would tell him for certain. I asked what is this? (Truly, I was ignorant.) He ordered more Vicodin for me, and we went home to await approval for the test. I am having intense trouble sleeping, and any position, I am in terrible pain. I am getting only 2 or 3 hours of fitful sleep. Then I hobble around and pace to try to get away from the endless pain. How did this happen? I was in such terrific shape.

December 4, 2003

I am waiting for the MRI approval from my HMO health insurance. Got approval for the test for tomorrow. Sleeping a lot, in great pain. I have no feeling in my left leg from the upper thigh to the foot. It is numb to the touch like it is drugged. The thigh muscle is one major knot and hard like a piece of wood. Pain is horrible and blinding at times. This has got to go away, I am in a bad spot, and I need to get back to my company. This is a bad time for this to happen. Every night now I can't sleep. This is getting bad … too much discomfort. I am able to write this in my journal, in fact, I use a handheld to do this as I am laying down so much.

December 5, 2003

The pain is awful. My leg is so bad and hard to move. I cannot feel anything from the knee down at all. I can move my toes and ankle, but the leg has no feeling, except for intense pain. We went to the MRI center in Orange for the test. We waited for the films. Darla drove me there and back. It was hard to sit and it was very exhausting to be out like that. Jamie called from Dr. Hanlon's; they received the report on stat from the center. He set the appointment for Monday to see Dr. Hanlon.

December 6, 2003

It is now the weekend and everything is the same as before, pain and discomfort. On Sunday I finally rested fitfully after another sleepless night. I am like a druggie now with sunken eyes and very irritable. Not eating well and getting constipated.

December 8, 2003

Monday the eighth, my appointment with Dr. Hanlon, he looked over the films. It showed a major rupture at the L4-L5 vertebral disk. Over 19 mm in size, going up the spinal canal in a caudal direction all on the left side. Dr. Hanlon says this is the largest rupture he has ever seen. He said this would require surgery, so he referred me to a neurosurgeon. He then said that I went from a disaster last year with the fractured left transverse process right into a catastrophe.

I left Dr. Hanlon, dazed. But Darla took me to see Dr. Edwards, my family doctor, due to the fact that the hospital ER doctor could not get a pulse in my left leg. We went to see

Dr. Edwards to see if my leg numbness was vascular related. Dr. Edwards checked this out and said my pulse is normal. We talked about the injury, and he said the neurosurgeon I will see is a very good one. I am in such great pain still.

December 9, 2003

Another day of waiting! I cannot work because it is too painful to sit. I can't drive due to the narcotics I am on; this is bad, and I am confused and upset. Why did this have to happen? The people at Dr. X's seem competent, but now I wonder. How could a trained doctor, using a major piece of thoroughly tested equipment, cause such a traumatic injury? I am in a bad way, and I don't have any answers. I am taking too much Vicodin, causing side effects. I am getting in a bad temper and I am having pains going to the bathroom! Man, it hurts to pee!

December 10, 2003

I am up early as usual waiting for my appointment with Dr. Schnitzer, the neurosurgeon, later today. I have been resting in pain; it's what I do now. My company needs me to run the business and assist in selling work. I am getting depressed with all this waiting.

Meeting with Dr. Schnitzer, he reviewed the MRI and examined me. He recommends surgery to remove the large disk fragment at L4-L5. He set the date for the twenty-third of December as the soonest possible surgery date. He also set up an epidural shot to be done to help with the swelling of the nerve compression. He seems to be a very confident surgeon.

December 11, 2003

Daily diary is the same, hard to sleep, irritable, on narcotics. Trying to work from home and contribute as I can. I can't sit up long periods, as it hurts too much. Resting a lot, I feel what a waste now, all that training. I was in such good shape, putting on new muscle from the trauma and had lost the weight I put on after the quad accident a year ago. Rick is such a terrific trainer, what a shame!

I type this into my PDA, and it is tough to do. Another day I will spell check. Sleeping sucks, no way to stop the pain, waiting for the 23rd to come and get back to work after short recovery. Pain is so bad I am jacked up. Darla is worried, hard to get close to her and we are having no relations. Is this due to my depression? Hers?

December 15, 2003

Friday the twelfth to Monday the fifteenth, diary is the same as before. Hard to sleep, am on narcotics, irritable. Trying to work from home to get as much done before the surgery. I have spoken to a neighbor who had a laminectomy surgery. This is what I am having done, I think. She said it was a snap, in and out in two hours; spent one night in the hospital and had no pain or numbness after the surgery. This is encouraging. On Vicodin, I can't wait for the beginning of this saga to end. This makes the ATV accident look tame. How can a squashed nerve create such hellish pain? My leg is all paralyzed and numb. How long will this take to heal? Prepped for tomorrow's epidural shot, no food or drink after midnight.

December 16, 2003

Went to a local hospital for the epidural shot. A Dr. Lee did the procedure. A good doctor. Explained everything well, had a bit of trouble at the first location. He switched and the next time it worked fine. Felt like getting stung by a big bee. After this Dr. Jacobsen walked with me and checked me out to be sure I was okay. He said he numbed my leg nerves so I should not have pain.

But by the time we got to the waiting room my leg was in great pain. He said, "Well, friend, you are going to have a humdinger of a surgery because that fragment is one huge piece. Going to make a neurosurgeon's day." I didn't laugh at this, I felt uncomfortable after the shot. I felt queasy and had very weird feelings.

December 18, 2003

Wednesday after the shot, odd day for me, I had spasms throughout my leg and back after the epidural shot. On Thursday the eighteenth, I was feeling better. I think I can move without my crutches since the leg is not as numb. Went to see Dr. Edwards for my pre-surgery checkup, and had an EKG done, X-rays taken of chest, and a urine test. I spoke to Dr. Edwards about a second opinion, his read on Dr. Schnitzer, and what his opinion was.

He gave me his advice to go forward and get this done ASAP. My symptoms are high trauma and require quick remediation. He wouldn't wait if it were his back. I thanked him. He has been a good doctor to me for the past ten years. I can see he is worried.

December 19, 2003

Went back to a local hospital to do paperwork and had blood work done. Bonnie drove me. Came back with Darla, all is ready it seems for next week. Seems a snap when you talk to medical people, some confusion though on the EKG, but it worked out. I am sapped, and I would like to rest and go tonight to our company party.

We went to the party, and I loaded up on pain meds. I sat in the best chair at Bob and Diana Johnson's, felt the best since the injury happened. The epidural must be helping. Dr. Lee had said it takes two days for it to kick in; must be reducing some swelling on the nerve.

What a great party, presents for the kids, good food. What great fun it was seeing our people out of uniform. Had the gift exchange, what a blast. Gave Bob and Diana the Dale Earnhart jackets I had bought in Las Vegas as a thank you. They cried, it was neat … came home I am so wiped out, but I needed this time to be with others and get my mind off my situation.

December 22, 2003

Began to prepare over these last days for the surgery on the 23rd, eating light meals, taking light laxatives to help with the upcoming constipation problems. A day of rest it is Sunday. Still in pain the nerve is back to being a pain, it is better at times. I am getting nervous about the surgery, thinking about the results. Stopped eating or drinking on Monday night or to get ready for the surgery tomorrow, really nervous now and in pain. The leg is numb and the thigh a big knot of spasms.

SURGERIES

December 23, 2003   **Surgery #**1

The big day has arrived. We arrive at the hospital and completed the paperwork. I got moved into an outpatient room for prep work. Surgery is scheduled for one o'clock. Doctor Schnitzer is late, so we stay in this room until past one. I got wheeled into the surgery center; got prepped with IV and stuff. Dr. Schnitzer arrived at one thirty and we go into the room. I was out about two PM

Surgery was supposed to last one and a half hours according to Dr. Schnitzer. It took over four and half hours! Dr. Schnitzer explained he removed large fragments of the disk going caudally up the spinal canal two levels. He had to remove a large section of my lamina spinal bone to access the canal. He spent a great amount of time in moving the nerve to expose all the bits of fragmented disk and to make a large window so he could get to all the areas where the disk had exploded to. He is a very thorough surgeon, and I am confident in his skills.

In the recovery room, I still felt numbness in my left leg and very groggy from the anesthesia, and went to my room. Missed dinner, it is like eight o'clock. Had nibbles of Jell-O and ice cubes; the nurses are great here, asked for and got morphine shots for pain. Rested with my family and tried to adjust to the incision in the lower center of my back, having difficulty lying down. Watched TV and had the nurses coming in to take my vitals every hour. Got up to pee, nurses helped get me there. *Wow! What intense pain in the back!* Couldn't pee, went back to bed, and could not sleep.

December 24, 2003

Wednesday the twenty-fourth, Christmas Eve, midnight, now just four hours since getting to the room. Since I couldn't pee, we went for a walk in the ward. This was slow but it helped, I am in *great pain*. Back to the room in bed, sitting up is the most comfortable, using the bed at a 45-degree angle. I cannot sleep, I ask for pain meds every couple of hours. The nurses are great.

It is now three AM Did I doze for a short time? It's hard to tell. *Pain* is there, and it is not stopping. My leg is in killer pain similar to the day of the injury. It is now near six AM, more tests and vitals and morphine shots. Breakfast around eight AM It is good, but I am not hungry. I could go home. Let's see what the doctor says.

It is now about ten AM Dr. Schnitzer came in, and we discussed the symptoms, which are the same. He says we must wait two to three weeks to do an MRI because the area is so swollen; until then I must deal with the pain. He said I could go home once I have a bowel movement. He said to call him if anything changes. I am walking every two to three hours in spite of the pain, which makes it very hard to rise up from the bed. I mean it is like every muscle is cut, and they are screaming at *me*!

It is now three o'clock in the afternoon. I am okay to go home, so Dr. Schnitzer gets the discharge orders and Darla comes and gets me. I insisted she stop to get a pillow from a store as I need to protect the back incision because it is painful. I actually went into the store on my crutches and picked out a fine pillow to sit on and use for my new style of life. It is nice to be home on Christmas Eve. Even though we have not been able to prepare with the tree and gifts since all this hospital stuff, appointments have been the priority.

I am now home and set up on the couch. Taking Norco, a stronger version of Vicodin. Hannah decorates the tree; Johnny is planning on seeing Santa. Darla is exhausted and goes to bed by 7 PM I am up but cannot sleep; the pain is extreme, but I guess this is to be expected since surgery was yesterday. How did Gamble's surgery differ from mine? One hour versus four-plus and major bone removal? I hope this pain goes away soon.

Now it is late, the kids are asleep, and I am watching TV. No gifts to wrap for me, as I could not go shopping. I have cards and stocking stuffers only. I am really feeling bad, but I am home and this is Christmas Eve. What a one to remember!

Christmas Day, Thursday the 25th

Ho, ho, ho. I wake up Darla to wrap the last gifts for the kids. They are asleep, I set up our camcorder, and Darla goes back to bed. The kids are up now and ready to go. Great excitement, it is good. We are all up now. I am in great pain! It is increasing, not diminishing. We open gifts; I look awful and feel worse. I am sobbing uncontrollably for my condition. This is not a happy Christmas for our family.

The kids are excited. Bonnie is in New York so we taped the gift opening for her. *Wow*, I am in a bad way; I know I am in great pain, but I am so immobile. We clean up, and I go back to bed. My leg is on fire with pain; better call Dr. Schnitzer; we page him. He calls back.

He prescribes methylprednisolone, a steroid. Darla finds a pharmacy open on Christmas Day! *Wow*! I take six pills to get started. I try to rest, but on Christmas this is impossible. The kids and things are happening, left and right. I am not doing well because the pain is tremendous. Constantly popping the pain meds as often as I can, I am up to 160 mg of codeine a day; the max is like 80 mg. The pain is tearing through my body and my leg like it is the first day; something is wrong. Sleep is broken and pain makes it tough to find a zero pain position, why, oh, why?

December 26, 2003

The pain is the same as yesterday. The pain is destroying my mind and spirit for this normally happy time. I am in too great a pain. I should be doing better. This isn't what my friends (Mac and Gamble) told me about their back surgeries. Something must be wrong. I am taking the pain meds like candy, two to three Norco's every 3 or 4 hours. It is just barely cutting the pain but when it shears through it is like a knife cutting my leg.

At last I get sleepy from all these meds or the effort to sustain. I get three hours at a whack, which is okay for me for now. As the day goes on into the afternoon, it's more of the same, a very bad day of pain. Now I am fully constipated and, wow, does it just kill to have a bowel movement. I don't feel like eating, and since the injury have lost over eight pounds.

December 27, 2003

Today is Saturday, more of the same, no pain resolution. This is incredible; the pain is like it was before. What could be wrong? I trust Dr. Schnitzer; he is a real surgeon's surgeon. You can tell from his focus. He also goes the extra distance by taking time to explain all that is happening. I am taking pill after pill.

It is now five PM, no sleep and constipated, what a hell's fury on the body as an added insult. Can't our American labs come up with pain meds that don't bind you up? Poor back sufferers. The nights are like I am living wired, I am doped up, yet cannot sleep, except for short naps. My sleep is broken up due to the pain of any position I am in. Incredible. I also have frequent bouts of sobbing for no reason—a word, a name, and a TV show where someone gets hurt, and I am sobbing. My hands shake with a tremor at intermittent intervals. What is happening to me?

I feel like I am cracking up as well as having this shearing pain in my left leg. The leg gets waves of pain like the bone has just broken and the brain-numbing pain associated with that. I had broken my right ankle 14 years ago and I remember that pain and the snap of the bone and the wave of excruciating pain. This is just like that, only it comes on and won't stop.

December 28, 2003

I can't take it. No sleep at all, maybe three hours. Pain is wild; I am wild! We called Dr. Schnitzer, and he ordered an MRI for tomorrow of the left leg and back, thank God. He ordered this on stat, he said to call Toni in the morning. A little hope goes a long way. Pain still raging though the leg!

I have been writing what is happening. I have shredding pains in my leg. It is numb from the knee past the foot. The thigh is like a giant knot of muscle and in constant pain. I cannot walk without assistance: I must use the crutches, and I am really not doing well here. I have hope now with the new MRI. This waiting and suffering is maddening for a fairly strong-willed person with a high tolerance to pain.

I pity anyone who experiences this … for me it is mind numbing and at times you wish it would just go away! Endurance is truly a test of a man's soul. I am surely being tested to the limit of my will and soul.

December 29, 2003

Toni called from Dr. Schnitzer's, the MRI is approved. Called the OIC to arrange for the stat appointment. I called and got the run around from a secretary. This can't be possible. I called Toni back. The stupid person at this OIC just made me angry and now my nerves are raging in pain. The insensitivity of people who are in the healthcare field, they need to go through this to be compassionate!

Jamie called later to apologize. He said everything is handled, and please come in around three PM Finally the MRI is done on the leg and the back, this one with no contrast. Had great pain having to lie flat on my back on the stiff table; also the ride in the car from home to Orange and back. Got home and took meds and passed out until the next MRI test tomorrow.

December 30, 2003

I awoke in the three o'clock hour in pain. How is this any way to exist? I have to find the meds but am groggy and sleepy, but awake due to the intense pain in my leg. Watched some TV and took the meds. I am going through these pills fast. I woke up, must have dozed again, and it is near six AM I took a shower. I can barely move the leg; it is so painful and numb. If it is hit, or I knock it on a table or chair or whatever, there is shrieking pain. It is like a hundred thousand nerves are killed even when you touch it with just a little force. This is like a torture curse. Ate breakfast; not real hungry, fruit and cottage cheese. Took the meds, now I am taking vitamins. I was on good supplements prior to the injury and I stopped. Maybe this will help. Multivitamins and amino acids.

We drove to Orange for the next MRI with contrast (a metallic dye injected into your veins). During this procedure I went numb on the whole left side and my face. As the test ended I was faint, and the nurse and Darla sat me down. A doctor was summoned who came over and examined me. I suffered a dizzy time for 15 minutes or so. I must have had a reaction to the dye. We then drove straight to Dr. Schnitzer's office.

He looked the films over and expressed disbelief at the fact that another large fragment had ruptured at the L4-L5 disk. He offered to remove it or to allow me a second opinion. I told him waiting won't do anything, I am in great pain, and I told him I have great confidence in him. So I said to take it out. We set up the next surgery for January 2nd.

We then went to the pharmacy to get me more meds and Vistaril to help extend the codeine. We got home after six PM, and I took the new meds, shortly thereafter the new meds took effect and I went out. I awoke in the wee hours of the 31st, around 2 AM I was hungry and in pain from my leg. I was really groggy, ate some light food and watched some TV and took more meds and slept again.

December 31, 2003

It is now morning and everyone is awake this last day of 2003. I am worried about Bonnie in New York. I called her yesterday and she finally called back. I felt better. She will come home on the 2nd, the day of my next surgery. I have high hopes for this; all is well or will be well. I am on meds so for the first time on New Year's Eve I am legal to be under the influence of a controlled substance, just kidding. No alcohol for me, not even champagne.

Called to talk to friends and family. Judy starts her chemo treatments next week, since she has colon cancer and had her surgery a year ago. She has had a tough go this past year; 2004 has got to be better. Staying on meds to keep the pain level down. I am taking 160 mg of codeine a day; it is killer pain, my friends, non-stop pain.

Started watching the New Year's programs, especially the New York one. Looking for Bonnie at every shot of the crowd. Wow, over 500,000 people there! I tried calling her again, no answer, and no connection. It is a strange New Year's Eve.

January 1, 2004

Happy New Year to all! My kids are asleep; Darla is here and very sleepy. I am wide-awake because of the pain. Hurrah for 2004! Ditto day from yesterday. I was hoping for a New Year and new results. Tomorrow will be surgery #2. Meds all the time, I am being controlled by the pain. You have no choice but to succumb to it.

It is near midday now; the kids are having fun with the toys and the New Year's Day. It is fun to watch the parades like when I was young. I just wish this constant pain in my back and leg would subside. It is maddening and emotionally draining. Talked to my mother, she is so sad for me. She is so angry at the place where this happened. She says I must file a claim. I am confused on that one. I don't like to make things worse than it is. But my mother says this is a travesty; I will wait to see how I do after tomorrow. I love my mother.

January 2, 2004   Surgery #2

The day has arrived, and we are at the hospital for the second surgery. We did the paperwork and went to outpatient to await the surgery team. It is now one o'clock, déjà vu. Here comes the surgery team, went to surgery, felt very frail and weak. During the set up of the IV, a doctor nicked a nerve in my left hand.

My middle finger jumped like it had been shocked. It hurt very badly. The doctor tried again and finally got the needle in.

This surgery to remove the new fragmented ruptured disk took over four hours. Dr. Schnitzer had to open more of the lamina area in my vertebrae at the L4 to L5 area. This was to allow more access to get all the fragments left. He removed all but a small part (5%) of the nucleus of my disk. He also removed a large fragment of the outer ring too.

After all this, Dr. Schnitzer then worked on locating loose fragments. He and the team searched under the nerves on 2 levels. Finally a small bit of white cartilage surfaced and he seized it with his tool (tweezers) and pulled out a gigantic length of string-like disk material. At the end of this string was a large section of fragmented disk.

This was near the left foramen side of the L4 vertebrae. He said it was highly unusual for a piece to take this form and to drift out of the canal area. After this Dr. Schnitzer concluded there were no more loose fragments in the spinal canal or, as far as he could see, going out the nerve root. I woke up in recovery with extreme pain, way more than the first surgery, a level 9+. I received pain relief; I was too groggy to know what was going on.

It was now after 7 PM and I was moved to the room. I was awake with my family. I ate small finger foods with Darla and Bonnie. I asked for a morphine shot. At 7:30 a nurse named Randy gave me the shot. The pain is so bad, I just sobbed there in the bed because there was nothing the nurses or doctors could do. I am in incredible pain, the back feels so much like the bones and nerves are crushed. I didn't verify what type of pain relief the nurses were giving me. Later I found out that after Randy left, every time I asked for relief; disagreed all I received was 5 mg Vicodin.

No way was this doing anything. Dr. Schnitzer had left orders for injections of morphine every four hours. This did not happen. I suffered through the night, stayed awake and tried the best to keep off my back by lying on my side, sort of. Finally I fell asleep around 9 PM About midnight I awoke due to pain. Went to the bathroom and walked with a nurse. The leg has less numbness and pain; the pain in the back is very bad.

I asked for pain pills and that is what they brought. I am wide-awake and cannot sleep. This is when I wrote this record on the handheld.

January 3, 2003

I finally slept until six AM Got up, shaved, and walked in the hallway using a walker. Left leg is weak and hurts. Not sure if it is okay. Need more time to assess for sure.

It is now eight AM I am having new numbness in left leg and shooting pains in calf and thigh. What is this now? Sitting in bed, left leg is numb from mid-thigh to foot. Scale of pain is 9+. Got pain pill only. Dr. Schnitzer came in around 9 AM and explained the results of the surgery. This one was more extensive. He removed more bone in my spine to expose the entire nerve root over two levels. This is a first for him.

He scooped under the nerves and found hidden fragments in the cavity. He examined my leg and back; the back has major swelling. Left leg has numbness and pains like before. Dr. Schnitzer feels this is a positive sign. The extensive work around the nerves is the reason for these symptoms. He said I could go home after the injections are done. I asked what injections? He said morphine. I said I have had none except for after surgery.

He was dumbfounded. A mistake was made. I was supposed to have pain control. *Oops!* I asked if we could start now, and can I stay longer in the hospital to get my stamina back some? My leg is really hurting, and I am in great pain. He said no problem. I had lunch; the food here is good. I feel like I am losing muscle mass.

Went for another walk for four laps (1/4 mile) in the hospital.

Even with morphine shot the left leg is killing me. I got back to the room and crashed until five PM Nurse Lynn, my wife, and my mother agreed I should stay another night and continue the shots. My right-side ribs are in great pain now too. Nurse Lynn agreed. She called Dr. Schnitzer to advise of the ribs hurting; he agreed I am to stay. I am pale, and it is hard to breathe. I can't lift my right arm too high. It causes a sharp pain in the ribs.

I got another morphine shot from Lynn. Ate dinner, had a short visit with Darla and Mother. They left at seven PM I was tired and sleepy. I woke up at 9 PM in great pain, my left leg is now numb from the hip to the foot and I can't move it, it is so bad. At ten PM, I got another morphine shot since the Vicodins are not cutting it. I got up to walk another four laps. Managed to read and worked on diary. Pain is wild, but I guess I have to live through this one.

It is now midnight, I worked, read a book, and watched TV. Waiting for the next pain shot, I can feel the last one wearing off. Actually the pain is always there, even after the shots. At two AM I asked again for the shot. Finally went to nurses' station. They said Moe would come soon. It was now three AM before she came, and I had to call again. Pain is going crazy now. Moe gave me 10 mg of morphine. I will sleep maybe. I am concerned for my leg; this is different. Nurse Moe says I will need a higher dosage painkiller once I go home; I agreed.

After mid-morning I will check with the doctor.

January 4, 2004

It is now four AM I slept until six. I awoke, took a shower, shaved, and changed pajamas. I was thinking of Dr. Hanlon; I wish I could talk to him. I went for a walk. *Wow*. I ran into Dr. Hanlon! He was at the nurse station on my wing. We talked. He said Dr. Schnitzer is great, I agreed. He said my fragments are the biggest he has ever seen.

He hopes I will not become addicted to Vicodin for the rest of my life. This statement stunned me. Vicodin is not enough for me right now, morphine maybe. I finished my walk. Dr. Schnitzer came in. We talked and he reviewed my condition. With the leg symptoms continuing as before and getting worse each day, he wants me to stay in the hospital for pain control.

We discussed additional surgeries and the next step. First was to go two weeks to allow the swelling to subside, next have a new MRI taken, confer and perform a new laminectomy and a spinal fusion to remove any fragments as required. The quicker this was done the less chance for permanent nerve damage. Darla came in, and Dr. Schnitzer confirmed with her that I would stay at least through Tuesday to control the pain. At 11 AM I received another shot of 10 mg morphine in the left buttock.

One hour later I start having a new intense pain, a sharp pain in the lower left back like broken glass on the nerve, the pain is level 9+. Activity is lying in bed, this lasted about fifteen minutes. I stayed very still. Darla went to lunch and returned. We made a list of items I want her to bring. Nurse Lynn checked on me, she asked me to take a methylprednisolone pill. I did, and then we went for a walk around the wing and back to the room. I then had more shrieking pain in the leg; this was very bad, lasted about five or ten minutes. Traveling to the upper leg and down the inner side to the front of the calf/shin.

Lunch arrived for me: veggies and potatoes. It was hard to position myself to eat, and the left leg was getting worse each minute. It is hard to find a comfortable position now, the leg is pumping and swelling, this is not like before. Something is wrong again. I asked for another morphine shot and got it. Just keep these coming to help cut the pain. I tried to help by lying away from the left leg. The swelling in the back is in great discomfort with painful movements. I would like to rest, but it is too painful to sleep. It has only been two hours since the last shot, but I called the nurse for another one. She came with the shot. This time I had harsh pain in the upper front quadriceps area of the thigh. It lasted fifteen minutes, then a major spasm in the calf. Then a great lateral pain from the knee through the shin for another fifteen minutes, all the while it is throbbing in the quadriceps area.

Same pain level as before the morphine shot and located in the outer left leg throbbing, throbbing with extreme pain spikes like a broken bone. This is going right through the morphine like a tidal wave, with no break or relief, it is moving from area to area. I tried to rest, impossible. The kids came with Darla and we ate dinner. I walked them to the door. Then went for a short walk through the wing; my leg is throbbing and completely numb.

I went back to bed, got a phone call from Sunny, a friend of my brother, Harry. She is a trained medical professional. She evaluated the surgery, the care, Dr. Schnitzer's approach, and commented he was proper and conservative in his care of this situation. She approved of his methods while enduring a tough situation and maintaining great poise with my uncommon disk herniation, back and nerve symptoms.

I agreed. Sunny gave me great hope for a disk replacement surgery if needed. This really helped to strengthen and validate my belief in a light at the end of this tunnel. My business partner called with his wife on the phone. I explained the events and my struggles of this second surgery. They hope this is it and that there are no more fragments left floating. They will come by on Monday to visit. Got another morphine shot at eight PM My leg is killing me, level 9 pains. I hope for relief from this living torture as each hour is sucking my mental state of mind to a place of despair. I must be strong and endure, even during these moments of despair. I have had a full day and it is lights out, and at eleven PM I go to sleep.

January 5, 2004

I awoke in the four o'clock hour. I had a strange dream of people hiding in a room; I could feel them but not see them. Weird. My leg is throbbing from the hip to the foot. A sharp pain radiates down the outer calf; pain level is 8+. My back is 6+ and I feel tired even after my longest sleep of over five hours. I called for a shot, then got up, washed, shaved, and changed clothes. Just standing now has caused a great pain in the ankle and on top of the foot to the shin area. Nurse gave me the morphine shot straight into the left buttock. I should have some relief soon.

It is six in the morning; I am working on the diary, listening to the news. Left leg is numb and thigh is having high pain level, rear of calf aches constantly just lying in bed in semi-sitting position, using the hospital bed as a recliner. Talked to Darla on the phone. Nurse VJ came in; we talked about this new surgery and the constant high pain level in my left leg. A friend called so I took the phone, then VJ came back and Dr. Schnitzer called. She told him of my current pain level and he wanted to talk to me. So I hung up the phone. Then VJ came back in and said Dr. Schnitzer ordered a new MRI for today.

This is good. I am having bouts of despair for my future. I am angry about why this happened to me, the machine and why that doctor at the clinic had me test then follow-up with the exercise right then, which overcame my back and ruptured my disk. The other doctors and attendants had always told me not to do any back exercises after using the machine. Why me?

At eight AM I had another morphine shot in my left hip then breakfast came. After breakfast I made a toilet trip, things finally went better. So I took another walk in the wing. My leg is throbbing and the shin is on fire with pain. I cut the walk short and came back to the room to rest. I am dizzy and disoriented. Is this the effect of Valium? My brother called and we spoke for a short time; he wants to come tonight to visit. VJ changed my bedding;

she is very sweet. My foot hurts terribly; I wish this were over. I am becoming grim and weary of the constant pain. It drains all my positive energy from me. I am in unbelievable pain.

I hope whoever reads this doesn't think I am a chronic complainer; I am a pretty stoic, tough guy. This constant battle with nerve pain is relentless, no position gives relief. No amount of morphine is stopping it. Kirk came by to visit. I showed him the machine info and discussed surgeries. He is a loyal, fine friend. He also feels strongly I am due restitution for my injury. I so much wish to be out of pain.

Even on morphine, all the previous narcotics, and two surgeries, I have more pain now, and my body is changing. I am getting shaky nerves, and my mind is not sharp or focused. I pray for this to be over soon so I can restore my health and my mind. Any loss of mobility is understandable and can be adjusted to over time. It is the mental changes which are frustrating. My sharp mind was my most cherished asset. I feel diminishment of mental acuity. I hope it is a passing event. It is now 12:15 PM; I have received another morphine shot.

I rest and then at two PM the technician came in to do the MRI. He took me to a special trailer built with the MRI unit. This was a long test, another dual test, one with contrast and one without. I told the technician of my previous reaction to the dye. He said this dye is not the same. However, again, I had a strange reaction. During this test I had great shakes throughout my entire body while in the tunnel.

Laying on the hard surface was miserable on my back. I came back to my room and had weird sensations in my body and mind. That contrast is a powerful stimulant to me. I called VJ for another morphine shot and she came quickly with this injection. My leg is now pounding much more than before.

Kirk came back to pray for me. He is a good friend and through all these years since I first met him and hired him into the trade, he has had a strong belief and faith in God. He has been true to this all the time I have known him, a sincere man of faith. I am tired and not well since the MRI test; Darla and the kids came in.

We ate dinner together; this was a stressful time as the kids were antsy, and Darla and I got into it about my mother coming over. I asked her to leave so I could rest. I didn't need more stress. I love Darla, but we just don't communicate well at times. I am tired and after they leave I just rest wide-awake, waiting.

Some time goes by and Dr. Schnitzer came into the room, very concerned. He sat down and explained the MRI result showed a large mass at the L4 nerve root in the canal. It is a blood balloon that is called a hematoma. He said this is serious. This explains the pressure on my leg and the intense pain. As my heart beats the blood is expanding the balloon directly against my nerve in the canal and imposing extreme compression on the nerve itself. The balloon is pushing against the vertebrae wall and then redirecting against the nerve. He said he is scheduling immediate surgery for tomorrow morning! He appeared very anxious about a third surgery. He gently explained that he has never before had two surgeries with so many fragmented disk pieces scattered everywhere. He is an incredible surgeon, and I understand what he must be going through.

I expressed to him my complete faith in his skills as a surgeon and his team. We went over this procedure and the risks. With having had the two previous surgeries, he explained that my chances for requiring a long recovery and infection are very high. He then expressed the gravity of the location of the hematoma. It is so remote inside the canal that should he miscalculate in excising it and slice the nerve then this would result in permanent paralysis to my left leg.

I asked him what the chances of this are. He said how about

the chances of success? I said okay. He looked me straight in the eye and replied, "Ten percent."

I looked at him and said, "We don't have much choice do we?" He affirmed that. So I again expressed to him my faith in him. He then explained the options of enlarging the incision and exploring the left lamina area to look for more fragment pieces. I encouraged him to do this to be sure that there are not any floating pieces left.

He expressed again that this could add huge time to recovery because the hematoma is obvious. I insisted he consider this option. I told him I could handle a third surgery, but not a fourth. He replied, "Three surgeries in two weeks is unprecedented in back operations." He then agreed to this unorthodox lateral laminectomy. He said that this would happen tomorrow. I asked him to confer with Dr. Hanlon, he said he would, then he thanked me and left saying, "See you tomorrow."

It was now after eight PM; I called for another shot of morphine, which I was given, and then toward midnight the nurses took away all my food and fluids. They began to prep me for surgery. I got up during this time to walk, as the tension was sharp in my mind. The nurse brought paperwork for me to sign. I am nervous and write in my diary. I read some and then after midnight I asked for another shot of morphine, my one slim hope of relief from this torturous hell.

January 6, 2004   Surgery #3

I slept until around four thirty and woke up in great pain; the left leg was very swollen and numb as if all the blood was gone from it. The pain was over the top; I called for a shot. I got the shot about thirty minutes later. I worked on a letter in my diary and on my computer. My back hurts, and I am constipated, tried to go, but no way. The leg is throbbing so badly now with shooting pains all through my rear side. Even with the pain I went for a walk, actually more like a slow shuffle, down the hallway to help loosen up the bound muscles. I came back, read the paper, and rested; no breakfast, waiting for surgery.

Around eight AM I called for another morphine shot, the new nurse came immediately with it and administered it. I complained of a stomach ache on the right side of my ribcage. Toni, the nurse, brought Maalox to help me. She also put in a new IV on the left arm and saline solution to prepare for surgery. Having horrendous leg pain as always.

Waiting for the surgery, about nine AM I spoke to my mother on the phone, then my brother Harry. Then Darla came in, she helped me to shower, shave, and clean up, and we went for a walk and spent some time talking to nurse Denise about the surgeries. Went back to the room; the pain is beyond belief.

Then Denise the head nurse came in to talk about the confusion on the first night back from the last surgery and the mix-up on not getting morphine injections. She assured me this would not happen again. I rested in bed; standing makes the leg hurt worse now. The leg is so swollen, and the thigh is untouchable; it feels like it is going to explode. Waiting for the surgery nurse to arrive, finally about noon she came in and we went to the surgery center.

Met the "A" team again. This time no talking and jokes, in fact most of the team was crying as they wheeled me in. Not a pretty sight I am sure to have a man need to go through three back-to-back surgeries with no success. Everyone Darla and I spoke with that morning at the hospital said they have never seen something like this ever, period.

Lights out, then I awake in the recovery room, I snapped right awake and heard Dr. Schnitzer speaking to me, he seemed happy about the surgery. Oh my God, the pain is everywhere and it is like the first two surgeries, plus additional all at once. I cannot move there is so much pain, like level 10+++. Dr. Schnitzer must have really opened up the back and moved all the spine muscles, because I cannot think about anything but pain. I hear a beep-beep sound and a nurse, Ann, I think, kept asking me to breathe. I guess I am not breathing. I cannot think at all, and all I think is to let go and drift away where there is no more pain. This is all I sense in what is left of my mind, a slow arching of my thoughts away from the pain for the last time. Then this voice says, "Breathe, Mr. Beeson!" Then I unconsciously take a breath and the pain hits again. So I let go time and space to drift to the spot of no pain. There I made it. Wait a voice. "Mr. Beeson, breathe!" Again it happens, I scoop in a small amount of air and the pain hits. This keeps going on forever, in a never-ending rhythm of voice, drifting, breath, pain, drifting, no pain, voice. Over and over, a slow dance that there is no me, just this voice and air coming in to my mind.

Then a new voice asks, "Mr. Beeson, do you feel pain?" I nod, so now this goes on, pain? Nod. Pain? Nod. Over and over until suddenly I see her and she says, "Mr. Beeson, I am at 100 cc of Demerol which is the maximum." I feel that I cannot breathe and everything hurts. She is saying, "Mr. Beeson, breathe, please!" This is very hard to do. I really can't breathe. Then she says okay, and I feel movement, and it is five thirty, and now I am in my room.

I see Darla, Gamble, and Hector there. But it is like I am out of my mind. The room is so tall and the walls close in on me. Everyone's faces are so huge, leering at me. I am going out of my mind with fear. I cannot feel anything but these weird pictures and sounds. I am so drugged. Where am I? Then I hear voices and open my eyes, but I had shut them again to block out the faces everywhere and now all is normal.

I hear Hector and Gamble talking. I see Darla; she is next to me with Gamble. Dr. Schnitzer had been there and explained what happened. They tried to explain it to me, but I am so drugged and doped it is all a blur. They tell me the hematoma had formed over the L4 nerve after the second surgery. This was compressing the nerve worse than the disk was. According to Hector this was the first time in medical history this had happened. To me it's not too encouraging to make medical history.

I now have a tube draining the blood from the nerve area to a large container. Man, does this sting like a bee! This is keeping the blood from clotting in the canal. I am very drugged and tired. Bonnie and Naomi come in. Bonnie helped me by feeding me ice chips; my mouth and lips are like the Death Valley floor, so dry. Soon everyone left. Hector stayed to explain more.

This was incredible; three major back surgeries (each more than four hours long) in only 14 days! This is a new precedent he says in medical annuals. For me it is the machine of torture that started this, and now I am devastated with incalculable damage. I am so weak and pumped with narcotics. Nurse Shae came in and gave me a morphine shot at six thirty. This is just when the Demerol began to wear off. I started to have knife-hot pains in the area of my back around the drain and incision. Those shots only help to cut the pain to a level of 9 or 10. I am in worse pain and discomfort than ever. My leg is numb with no feeling and still throbs but the pain seems less. I wanted food; I was so hungry. Someone brought me some Jell-O and crackers. I feel so bad. I got up quick to use the toilet; oh my God, this is horror!

Nurse Shae and Violet came in fast; they watched me like a hawk. I made it back to bed and asked for another morphine shot, which I got. It is now like eleven PM, and I asked for a sleeping pill. I finally went down.

January 7, 2004

I awoke after maybe only two hours of sleep. The leg is numb but better. The pain has dropped to a level 8. I feel weak and nauseated. Must be the combination of morphine and Demerol. I worked on my notes using the Palm Pilot. I asked for another morphine shot. I got up to go to the bathroom, and again nothing happened. I was very wobbly and tired. I went back to bed and laid down to catch my breath, it is so hard to breathe.

Nurse Shae came in and checked my leg with a pin. No feeling at all from the mid-thigh down. Nothing. I spend the day in bed due to the fact that I am too weak to do much of anything. Not interested in food, I am just so sick and weak. Watched TV, read, but tried to sleep when I could. Kept asking for shots of morphine. Nurses coming in all the time to take my vitals; it is a nuisance, but important. My breathing is hard and my ribs hurt a lot.

In the afternoon Darla came by to visit. She said our partner called and is coming over to see you. We talked, and I asked about the kids and Bonnie. She said they are at home with Bonnie watching them. Now the worst is seemingly over. I agree. Darla is pleased with my nursing care and the great attention I am getting, and that I am doing as well as can be expected. This has been hard for her, and I know it is an emotional roller coaster especially to see your partner go through such pain. We haven't talked much about the future since we have been just taking things day by day.

My partner comes in by himself. He sits down with Darla and me and explains that our company has in the last forty-five days floundered without me. They need help and (his father-in-law) had a meeting at his home last night. He and his wife, who had loaned us money, were considering closing us down and taking the loss. He changed his mind and wrote a paper giving himself full authority to make all decisions as CEO for the company, and then he would infuse more money in the company. My partner had already signed it and handed it to me.

I took my time to think this over. I am in a horrible way, on drugs, morphine, and weak, just twenty-four hours post surgery and now this bomb in my lap: to give up the company to my partner's father-in-law. He called his father-in-law on the phone and handed it to me. He was mad that I hadn't signed. We talked—well, he talked and I just listened, considering I was so out of touch with the company. I said okay, like, what am I to do? They have me over a barrel.

I signed this paper and my partner left. What happens now? Only God knows. I am so wiped out I took another shot of morphine and Darla left. I sobbed for a long time …

DEPRESSION

January 8, 2004

It is now one AM; I awoke when Nurse Shae came in to take my vitals. I had slept from eight PM when I had taken two Vistaril, with a Valium, and some Vicodin to sleep. My leg after this rest is relatively comfortable. However, the shin is numb and the thigh is tight. Once I stood up and walked, the leg really throbbed and the shin is tight with numbness. I am wobbly on my feet.

I have not had a morphine shot since last night. I begin to have the shakes; I asked for another sleeping pill and more Vicodin. It is now about three AM I fall asleep. Around seven AM, Dr. Schnitzer came in and woke me up. I really slept! I showed him that the shin and knee have little feeling; he poked it with a pin and received no response. The rear of my calf has improved a little. My thigh is still hurting constantly, more so when I walk. The pain level is a 7.

He inspected the incision, and then we discussed my discharge. He said whenever I wish, no rush. I agreed to monitor my pain and strength. I am quite weak. He said that is to be expected. We discussed my recovery. He feels it will be three to four months before I can return to work. He then discussed with me Artificial Disk Replacement (ADR) surgery versus fusion surgery. He said if I wait two years ADR will be here in the USA and then I should do that instead of a fusion due to my age and good condition (formerly). I don't know too much about all this; I hope I can make it two years.

The rest of the day I sleep off and on, just taking Vicodin throughout the day and into the evening. Another night is spent in the hospital.

January 9, 2004

I wake up early after a fitful night of broken sleep from the nurses taking vitals, etc. I am walking now and taking loops around the wing. The leg is still numb, but less pain. My back is painful but getting tolerable.

I watch CSPAN; a morning broadcast about a guy named David Cay Johnston and his book *Perfectly Legal* that is on the IRS or something. It sounds very interesting, so I write down the info, look it up on the Internet and order it. I've got to have something new to read to help me through the long recovery. It is another day here, and I am feeling stronger, not as weak, not terrific but better. I am coughing a lot and my ribs hurt, but it is the best for now.

Dr. Schnitzer came in to see me, and we talked about the status of my leg and back. He feels my prognosis is better since this third surgery, no more radical symptoms! We are now into recovery, and I have not even had a pain pill since yesterday. He is hopeful this is a good sign. He thinks I look good after an exam and he decides to release me home! He prescribed Vicodin, Vistaril, and Valium for home. I am happy and elated!

I am still coughing, but this is okay. Darla comes with the kids to pick me up. I am very excited!

We went to the pharmacy to get the prescription while I waited in the car because I am tired. I also got the shakes again, so when Darla came back with the meds I immediately took some Valium to ease the pain and relax me. Oh, it is heavenly to be home. I go right to bed. What a joy to be home and in my own bed!

January 10, 2004

I awake Saturday morning around seven AM, and I'm coughing a bunch more, but I am happy to be home! What an ordeal this has been! The worst is over and now on to recovery for, what, three months, then back to work part-time? Will three months do it? I thought eight weeks for each surgery, and I had three so it would be more like six months to recover, who knows? When I do something, I do it well.

I am in pain but I am tolerating it now. I have lots of meds to take, and I can cycle the stuff to cut the pain. My leg has improved from what it was before the third surgery; this is something I plan not to repeat. I wonder how many people have ever experienced that. Not many, I am sure, maybe someone who has been burned badly and has non-stop escalating pain. Well, it seems to be behind me now.

I am home and now can get my life back. I am sure I can start to move some and go for walks to make my muscles heal faster. And I can take supplements too. Vitamins, etc. But just to be able to sleep undisturbed without having vitals taken is wonderful. Darla seems relieved; this has been tough on her. She looks dragged out, like after a weeklong bender or something. She could use a Valium too.

Oh, what pain it is to walk! I will take it easy today and plan a walk tomorrow. I am taking twelve Norco a day and Vistaril. I have to make it on this. Breathing is hard, I may have caught a cold at the hospital due to the thin blankets they have there.

January 11, 2004

Today is Sunday; I woke up coughing deep from the lungs, and it is hard to breathe. I dressed and went downstairs and had to sit to catch my breath for about 15 minutes. I did the physical therapy on legs following the hospital's instructions. Laid down for about two hours, then got up and took a short walk outside using my cane. Came back and rested more. Very tired and coughing persistently, getting shakes and a great pain in the right ribcage. Took cough syrup to help the cough due to it being so painful. Just very tired today, far more than the last two days, discussed these concerns with Darla.

Ate a light lunch, watched TV, and read. Bouts of coughing, feeling weaker, and getting the shakes in my hands. Rested and would like to go out, maybe that would help. Later Darla said she needed to go out; I need a proper size cane. So after a while Darla and I went to the store, I got dizzy after just a few minutes and went back to the car and rested. We went home. I am very tired now, ate a light meal and rested. I am drinking lots of water and taking vitamins, etc.

I am coughing now all the time; it is very painful and I cannot breathe very well. I need help. We called Dr. Schnitzer and he called right back. We told him of the right rib pain, shortness of breath, feeling weaker, and the coughing. He said to go to the emergency room. So we did. Darla took me back to local hospital. I was very weak and disoriented. After being seen in the ER and stabilized with a DiLaudid shot, a much stronger drug than morphine, they put me on oxygen, ran an EKG, and took CAT Scans and X-rays. I guess they are looking for abnormalities or embolisms. I was admitted to the cardiac wing for observation.

Tomorrow the floor doctor will see me for additional work up. I am very weak, tired, and my breathing is shallow. Nurse Charone is assigned to me. She sets up sensors on me to monitor oxygen and my heart. Asked about my pain level. I say the ribs are a five, the back a three, and the leg a three. She offered pain meds but I never got any. I called for a sleeping pill about midnight and got a Vistaril and a large aspirin, no pain pill.

January 12, 2004

It is now Monday, about four in the morning. I was awakened by Nurse Charone to take my vitals. My blood pressure is 100 over 60. Went to the bathroom. She gave me a container to use. She came back to help me to bed, I am so weak. She asked about my pain level. I said a five. She said she would bring a pain med. It is now five AM, and I am still waiting. Started coughing from the lungs, a deep ragged cough, makes the ribs burn and hurt. At five thirty I finally got morphine shot into the IV.

A new nurse named Nana comes in about seven AM; shift change I guess. Very fast-moving gal, came in, checked my vitals, and checked the oxygen. Still coughing hard, the lungs and ribs hurt really badly. Breakfast came with a newspaper. Feeling better than last night, I think it is the oxygen helping. A Dr. Kim came in and examined me. He said the alveoli sacs were closed in my lungs from the lack of deep breathing due to all the surgeries. He ordered a nebulizer and a float treatment, and he is keeping me in the hospital. This is a collapsed lung!

A nurse named Mel came in soon and began the first nebulizer treatment with oxygen and a chemical to help break up the closed sacs. This lasted about ten minutes. Then she showed me the float lung exerciser. I have to inhale and exhale with this float every hour for ten minutes. I started at the 1200 mark. Then you finish with a deep breath to induce coughing to clear the fluids. Man, this hurts like your ribs are busted or a muscle is torn. I am very weak still from this lung collapse; I hope this stuff works fast.

Lunch came, not bad. Mel came back after that for another nebulizer treatment. The chemical tastes like ashes. Then I did the float and coughed my guts out using boxes of tissue. Every hour: float, cough into tissue, ditto, ditto, and ditto.

About three PM I started having stomach cramps. Went to the toilet, but I am constipated again! I called Nana; she said she would bring me some prune juice and a pain med. Then she told me I am to be moved to the surgery/med ward, my old home. While waiting for Nana to come back the cramps became diarrhea, just like that! After this Nana came back with the prune juice, I laughed. Then she prepped me for the move to the 200 Wing.

I am now in room 228A. Nice room, Randy is my nurse, the same as last week. He couldn't believe I was back again. He left to do his rounds and I had more diarrhea. This is strange, I asked for a pain med and water. I worked the float every hour and, of course, had raging coughing afterwards. I got pain pills, no shots. They also stopped my oxygen. A nurse named Dan came in and did another nebulizer treatment. I then did a float and again coughed up tons of fluids from my lungs.

Darla came in; we went for a walk and saw VJ, Kim, and the other nurses. They were amazed that I was back and looking so frail and weak. We looked around, went back to the room, and dinner came. I shared it with Darla. Still more float to do, I am up to level 2000. I asked for a pain med from VJ, and she gave me a morphine shot. What a sweetie! My leg pain has gone up from this new mess. I guess from the fact I am so weakened from this lung deal.

Float, coughing, tissue, float, coughing, tissue, ditto, ditto, ditto! Now I am getting the same meds as before, morphine and Valium. I need to sleep, more float work and inhaler. More coughing and more coughing, the pain in the ribs is terrible; I am so weak and tired from this. I finally slept some, not sure how long because I wake up to cough and float and use boxes of tissues.

January 13, 2004

I woke up, and it is Tuesday the thirteenth, about five AM I am weak, but breathing is somewhat better. I used the float, more coughing and rib pain. VJ came in; she will be my nurse today, good. Asked for a pain shot, no problem. She came right back and gave me one. Took my vitals, listened to my lungs. Breakfast came, and then Mel found me and did another nebulizer treatment. She says I have improved greatly!

Keep doing the float, she says; I am, I reply. My breathing is better, but I am so greatly weakened by this new ordeal. My leg pain is not forgotten, it is very severe again. Dr. Schnitzer came by and we talked about the lungs. He is glad I came straightaway to the ER. He seems very concerned about my lungs. He discussed my leg pain and checked the incision area. We talked about another MRI because of the leg pain. He wants to wait another six weeks before we do it to let the swelling subside. He told me to call Toni to set our many postoperative appointments.

Lunch came. After lunch, more float work, more coughing, yet I am now hitting 2250 on the float scale. Mel came in and did my last nebulizer treatment and float. A technician came and we went to have new X-rays of my chest. I came back to the room and found that Ray Scott, my friend and counsel for my company, came in to see me. He is a very sincere man and a devout Christian. I do enjoy our visits, especially when it doesn't cost me anything; just joking. He prayed for me, and that again is a powerful statement for one man to do for another man. It shows true compassion in the name of God. At this time I thanked him for his friendship. He discussed with me the aspect of filing a claim against the doctors for my injury and the timing of statutes if I should decide to file. I am so confused as to this matter. On top of all my pain I am in, it is too much to think about.

Dr. Kim came in and examined my lungs and breathing and pronounced I could go home! I called Darla and asked her to come get me. It is the afternoon. Darla arrived, and then we waited for VJ to get the orders, remove the IV, etc. A short time after this was done, we left for home! What a feeling to go home! Once there I took my pain meds and a sleeping pill and went to lie on the couch; I was so tired. Then John, Hannah, and Charley, our new dog, came in. He is a Lhasa Apsos breed, very sweet and possessive, that Bonnie had purchased last summer from its previous owner. The kids just love him, and he has adapted to us very well. They are happy to see me again. It is so wonderful to have this reception.

I am really tired, watched TV and made phone calls to my mother to let her know I am home and to Carol. They had gotten confused because I was still at the hospital last weekend and really became worried. It is getting near nine PM, so I take a Valium to get some rest. I am very weak and have a low stamina level, so I went to bed.

January 14, 2004

I awoke about eight AM and took a shower, oh yeah, it is nice to be at home and to sleep without the disruption by nurses doing their job to be sure your vitals, etc., are fine. Oh, the joy of home! I cleaned up the sensor adhesive and yuck from the past few days and got dressed. My leg hurts and is throbbing, but I would like to go for a walk and start my rehabilitation exercises.

I took meds with laxatives and lots of water. I went for a walk, almost a mile. Wow, this was tough! I am so winded, and the leg hurts badly on the front shin. It is good to be outside, but now I am concerned about my poor stamina and damage to my lungs. I wonder if I can get oxygen for home. I came back, lay down and worked the float and breathing. I took my blood pressure; it is 126/74, pulse is 87, not bad for a drugged-out, hacked-up, winded, and ancient-feeling young man!

I talked to my mother and sister on the phone to give them the update on my status. Did more floats and coughing, exercised my lungs then had a light lunch. The leg is calming down from the walk. It took over three hours for the pain to subside. I am trying to lighten up on the meds, it has screwed my intestines into a knot, and I am constipated again. I still can't get over this last hospital stay and the diarrhea I had right after being constipated.

I keep working this float tube, a plastic vial that has a hose and a float. You have to blow/inhale into it and watch the float sensor rise to a certain level and then you have to keep it there while exhaling. It is hard to do the higher you go. I am at 2250. You have coughing fits right after and major phlegm comes out of your lungs, and it is so painful. I am glad that I did not contract pneumonia while this happened, that would be worse I am sure. Yet my lungs feel torn. I am sure it will take a while for my ribs to heal. I feel like a mule has kicked them in whenever I have coughing fits. I can still barely lift my right arm up as it tears the ribs on that side with massive pain spikes. Suffer through more float, coughing, tissue, ditto and ditto.

It is now afternoon and the kids come home from school. Lots of activity having a seven- and eight-year-old girl and boy hit the house after a day at school. A flurry of action is going on here, there, and everywhere. The phone here rings a lot with calls from family, friends, and business folks, even vendors. I am not up to all of this right now and it shows on my stamina level, which is close to negative.

Darla talked about the meeting with our partner at the hospital and the company debt load with his father-in-law putting pressure on us, as I signed a note to him securing the funds. Darla is angry at the debt I have exposed her to from this. I am too weak to respond right now.

I keep working the float, still haven't taken any meds. I'm trying to help my stomach and get away from the effects of the drugs. I am not getting much rest, too much happening: phones, dog barking, kids in and out, cell phones on and off with sounds and all. It is not good.

I ate dinner, stayed on the couch, too tired to go to the table. After this the kids were hard on homework time. I am not well. Doing float and coughing up tons of fluids, and I am weak. Darla and I talked about having a broker handle selling our motor home, as I can't do much with it. The broker wants to come by on Friday to pick it up. He had come and seen it and worked up an estimate for $16,000. We could sure use this money.

More float work, more fluid coming up from my lungs, and more pain. I am getting really tired and take a Valium to calm me down and sleep. I counted my meds and I am taking 12 to 15 Norco a day, and I thought I was cutting back! I am sickened by this! When will it stop?

January 15, 2004

It is now about two AM Finally, the house is quiet. I got up and watched some TV, worked on my diary and worked the float. Lungs still hurt, but I can now get to the top of the float. Working it very consistently every hour on the dot. I read some and worked on email. I can't sit up very long; my back just kills me. My leg and calf will either spasm or the pain just intensifies. I am trying to rest the pain away and not take Norco. I take a Valium instead.

It is like five AM, Charley gets up, and I let him out to do his thing, a smart and quick little guy. I give him a treat when he is done and this becomes a habit. He lies around all day long mostly, unless the doorbell rings, and then he goes berserk. I worked on email some more, actually tried to figure out this new Palm software and get my old Palm unit downloaded from it failing. Thank goodness I had Darla bring me my computer at the hospital and I backed it up, or I would have lost everything I had recorded. Another frustration on top of my misery is all this computer stuff that fails at the wrong times.

More float work and coughing. It is now seven AM, and soon the kids will be up. Darla comes down, and we get into a major argument about the company, the meeting last week, and her part of the debt. I guess she has been stewing on this, but I am so whacked out right now I am shaking, and my nerves are blown. I told her she is no respecter of people and that even though she has been considerate of me in my condition this is unconscionable, attacking me when I am really down. I am very angry and shaking, I throw a cup, and man, I have to get out of here, now. Maybe I should move out, this is bad.

Maybe I will take the motor home and drive it to a park and stay there. Darla goes to work, and I take some clothes and belongings and pack them up. I fall down in exhaustion; I am so messed up in pain, and now emotionally wiped. *Wow*! Why does this have to happen? Marriage, life, stupidity? I slept quite a while to let out this bad energy. I am furious. If I were well I would be out the door.

I find my keys and take my truck for a short drive, I am so nervous. I go slowly and drive to a park close by that I thought takes RV's but they don't. But it is nice to day camp. I drove some more, just needing to sort my thoughts out. What a blow! I am shaking fiercely, and I have been out a couple of hours so I come home and take some Vistaril and Valium and lay down to sleep. I slept, but I had a bad dream that people were chasing me, and I was crippled and couldn't do anything. I awaken and think about Darla. We have great differences on money and communications; we do well as a family, parenting, and just the two of us. Maybe we are not as close since John and Hannah came. That has been a big load on her along with me leaving a good position to go into business.

Yes, this is my company and requires my time. How that will shape up as I recover, only time will tell. I have worked as hard as three men to build this business into a multi-million dollar concern in a short time. And yes, it has struggled; many growing companies struggle and then settle in. We have only been doing this for four years, and we have had insane growth with pains. Yes, we owe a bunch of money and it is poignant right now with this terrible time. But Darla has shown her complete disbelief in me and in this business.

January 16, 2004

It is now Friday. I wait until Darla is gone to work, and I go out and check the motor home, start it, warm it up, and drive it down the street. I went to the gas station to top the tanks and realize I'm not confident in handling this in my condition. I will have to reflect on this. I came home and parked it in front of the house. I am really at a low point in my life and depressed. I am sure Darla is too.

I have just been through the most telling time in my life with surviving three surgeries. She didn't. I pity her at times, yet I love her with all my heart and for all she does for our family. I know it hasn't been easy with the way it seemingly has been the last four years. Right now it seems this relationship is not healthy for either one of us. My concern is for the kids. We could sell the house and pay off our immediate debts and have some money between us, but will life be different? Happier? I am rocked with pain and emotions and really low.

I haven't walked since Wednesday. I am too exhausted, trying to use the float and work out the remaining fluids. My heart is crushed, and there is so much damage to my nervous system right now, I'm afraid of the future like no other time. It is near noon and I have lain down in the house to sleep as my pain level in the leg and back is nuts, too much stress I think. Trying to handle all this, and it is impossible.

I cannot walk far or even do my exercises. I am weak. I sure could use more oxygen; that stuff really helped me to clear the fence, so to speak. I am working on the float and can hit 2250 easily, so why am I so weak? I have, for all intents and purposes, stopped the meds. It has been ten days since my last surgery, yet I have little spark or stamina. Is the lung still collapsed? I have great pain in my leg, and I am trying to rest to keep the pain lower.

January 17, 2004

Today is Saturday. I woke up very late, near ten AM I am still very weak; the pain in the leg is increasing. Feels like the left leg is numbed out as if I had slept on it for hours. Yet I slept normally, not constricting it. I guess the nerve is getting moved or something. I can barely stand on it.

I ate lunch, an egg salad sandwich. Light fruit. I am trying to go as long as I can with no meds to see if I can stand the pain and resume my life. It is getting tough. The days have gone by in a fog, and I am not sure what is going on. Darla and I fought and now it is passed. What a cruel deal going through this and stressing us each to the maximum. This may break our marriage, which has endured through rough waters, but we always saw the sun shining. I just wish I were pain free—no, just half the pain would do.

January 18, 2004

It is now Sunday. God, this is terrible for one person to endure, having so much pain in my body. I am almost passing out. Darla came to me and said to either take the meds or she would call 911. So I started up and began the meds with two Norco, two Vistaril, and a Valium. Off and running back to narcotics. It has been a wild week. I am in a strange land right now, not sure I want to be here.

January 21, 2004

Today is Wednesday. I went to see Dr. Chan, who is Dr. Edwards's colleague, regarding getting oxygen. He examined me and noted my weakness but said my saturation level is 97 and it will be hard to get insurance approval for this.

January 23, 2004

It is now Friday and I have had high-level pain since yesterday in my left knee similar to a fire/burning sensation. My left ankle hurts like broken glass is in it. I took many Norco and Vistaril throughout the day. Ralph's guys came to get the motor home and on signing the paperwork I noticed Ralph and Darla had written it up as 1995, it is a 1990. The guys took the motor home and Darla called Ralph. They agreed to hold off, and Ralph will re-estimate the value. What a dumb thing!

January 24, 2004

Woke up and my lower leg feels like it has been hit by a sledge-hammer. Why does it have to be like this? I only slept three hours last night. I have to take more meds. I am hung up again in the intestines. God, this is a terrible affair. My back muscles get ripped apart due to the stress of constipated bowels, a narcotic side effect, even with the use of a daily laxative.

It is no use, I am hung up, my leg pain is making me sick, and

I am getting delirious. I take more meds, Norco and Vistaril. I let Charley out to do his thing; I am so envious of a dog's ease in going anywhere.

January 25, 2004

It is Sunday, and I woke up with massive calf pain, the same as when the disk ruptured! I took two Norco. I spoke to my partner's father-in-law this morning on the phone about the company. He will no longer help with money. I suggested selling the company to a larger company so maybe we could get enough money to pay him back and keep the business going with a new owner. He liked this idea. Even though a week ago he chewed me out for talking to our accountant about it. So now I will try to find a buyer, hmm.

I relaxed and read the current bestselling book while waiting for my partner to come by. He and his wife came. We did not talk about this plan. But he spoke to his father-in-law this morning too. They stayed a while and left. My leg was on fire so I took more Norco and Vistaril.

Later I took more, as the pain is the same. Ate dinner about six and still having high pain. Took more meds. Why isn't this working?

Watched CNN news, Darla brought in a new chair. It is an inversion style with a massage feature. We set it up and I put ice on my ankle and shin, took more Norco, and rested. Read, took more meds, watched some TV, and fell asleep.

January 26, 2004

Monday. Woke up very groggy with major throbbing in left leg, took some vitamins, and made breakfast. Leg is exceedingly painful, signed online to check emails, more depressing news about the company's money problems, so I laid down in the recliner with the massager on and read the rest of the *Da Vinci Code*.

This chair really helps to take the strain of my back pain away. When I stand the leg throbs and the ankle acts like it is broken. It is near three PM, so I took more Norco and Vistaril. Stayed in the chair; it is great. Darla does love and care for me despite of our struggles; I wish I could be more help to her.

Laid down on the couch about four PM; pills make me sleepy and with my leg so unstable I am prone to lose my balance walking. Watched the news on TV. Nothing good is happening, so I fell asleep. At seven I wake in pain and took more meds. Back to sleep.

January 27, 2004

It is early and I woke up to much pain in my bowels. Nothing happening there, just constipated again. This is so harsh; the pain to do this is terrible. It is like torture. I showered and got ready for my day.

Mac stopped by for about half an hour. I feel so out of touch with the company. He is a good friend and has been for a long time. I feel weak and have low energy. At lunch I ate a light meal, and rested. I took more meds and now a muscle-relaxing pill.

Read the paper, watched TV, and talked on the phone. At 3 PM the kids came home, what a shame I cannot do much with them due to my condition, this is so depressing. At four, I took more Norco, Vistaril, and Robaxin, the muscle-relaxing pill. Ate dinner, watched TV, at least the presidential primaries are on and offer some intelligent programs to watch. Fell asleep about nine after taking more meds.

January 28, 2004

My partner called. After this, Darla came in and we had another hard discussion about the company and decisions. My partner had asked me to take a cut in pay upon my return to work. I am no longer getting paid; they (the father-in-law) stopped paying me in the first month. I had set up a small loan to offset the loss until the disability payments kicked in. He is confused. I told my partner he could take the pay-cut and not pay me anything when I come back if he must. That made Darla angry with me. I took more meds with a Valium to settle me. My nerves are fried and I am close to a breakdown with the shakes and emotional fears. I slept until about four PM

My brother called; we spoke about the company. I told him about the conversation with my partner's father-in-law and asked Harry to inquire with large contractors to see if they had an interest in purchasing the business. We talked about me, and how I think it will be months until I will return to work. With my new leg pains another fragment could be the cause.

Friday, I meet with Dr. Schnitzer; he wants to do another MRI. We think he feels a disc replacement is the best option for me. I told all this to Harry. He asked for reports on the company, and he would call the investor. During this call I lost my emotional hold and started weeping; I told Harry goodbye and kept weeping for a long while.

All this business stuff is draining me, and I am so mentally exhausted from dealing with it. I fear the company is heading down the tubes, my partner and his father-in-law don't know enough about this business. His father-in-law has great business knowledge, but this service stuff is new to him. We are cash poor, have weak sales and weak management. I am no help and could be selling and inspiring the staff. If we find a buyer and get him paid back, and get good backing, we would have jobs for my partner and me. Well, I am not sure about me yet. I may need more time to recover from this trauma to my back and body.

Ate dinner, took more meds and Valium. The pain is so

numbing at times it overwhelms your brain. I am a tough guy, but with my stamina low and my nerves shot, the pain just hits with such intensity. If it weren't for the pain meds I would be thinking suicide, I am sure.

Dr. Schnitzer talked about scheduling level-two pain management; I will discuss it with him on Friday. I tried to go to the toilet and, oh, what misery! Constipation, even though I'm taking daily pysillium! The pain of this is so unbelievable no matter the meds, I cry out in agony. I wonder what new damage is being done to my rectum or to my colon. I know the drugs cause this, but I have tried to go without the pain meds and almost caused Darla to have a breakdown.

Dr. Schnitzer firmly instructed me to take the meds since the pain is so intense. After one of these episodes your blood is pumping fast, your body is shaking and weak, and your mind is thinking, *How will I survive another one of these in a day or two?* This is a terrible thing I am going through, why me? It is now late, so I took meds, a Valium, and went to bed.

January 29, 2004

Thursday. Woke up with a very stiff leg, the knee is having great pain that feels like a vice is squeezing it with tremendous force. The pain is fierce, level 8 or more. These pain meds just cut the pain. I stood up from bed, lost my balance, and fell. The leg is not stable. I massaged the leg and worked it so I could stand and walk. I am like a one-legged man; the leg is so stiff and painful. I cleaned up and shaved, made my way downstairs and fixed a sliced apple with peanut butter. I sat in the recliner with the heat on and the body massage.

Watched "Tale of the Gun"; kept getting up every half hour to walk around and check the leg. I am still having harsh pain at the calf and ankle, so I took more Norco, Vistaril, and Robaxin with a Valium. Watched TV and then fell asleep until 3 PM

Darla came home with Johnny and a new prescription for Norco, so I took some more of everything. The leg is so painful at the calf and ankle; it shoots down the sides of the leg and in the front the same as before the surgery. I don't understand this, but I am taking the meds now consistently to keep the pain at bay. I hope tomorrow Dr. Schnitzer helps to find the reason for the pain.

I know the numbness will take months to heal and for the spasms to stop. I am walking a quarter mile once a day. I have no stamina to do more than that. I have not done well since the third surgery and the collapsed lung event. I am having bouts of depression due to these setbacks and the other anxieties of life and my business.

Darla and I have had zip of a relationship. I am not much good to her in this condition. She is a woman with real needs and female emotions. She is young and needs a good man, not a busted-up druggie. I worked on my diary, called my aunt Marilyn, and spoke to Sark, her husband, ate dinner and took vitamins and had dessert. Watched TV: the History Channel on Disasters. It reminded me to measure my blood pressure, and it was 100 over 65, pulse 77. I will start to do this regularly.

January 30, 2004

Friday. I woke up with shearing pain over level 9 in the left leg tearing from the knee down the shin to the foot. Took more meds, they just cut some of the worse pain; it is still intense like a constant broken bone type pain. It is near three AM, so I lie back down to sleep. Darla woke me up. I am very groggy and took a shower. Pain is worse now on the outer calf and thigh area.

It is close to 1:30; I called Toni to confirm the appointment. Toni said it is for 2 PM, so hurry in. So we went quickly, Darla and I. Dr. Schnitzer came in and he reviewed his notes; he asked about my pain. I described the high level of left leg pain sending sharp shooting pains down the sides of the leg. I also explained I am weaker than before the lung problem. He asked me what has been done.

I told him that last week I saw Dr. Chan; he tested my saturation level and said I would not qualify for oxygen. Dr. Schnitzer feels this is a lung problem and wants me to see a pulmonary specialist. He feels the nerves are sending high pain shocks and the meds I am on will not handle this; I need higher-level nerve pain meds. We concluded I needed to see a PMD (Pain Management Doctor) and an MRI. I asked Toni for copies of the records of all the medical/hospital work and for a disabled placard application for parking. I told her it is too difficult to walk in from the parking lots into the places I need to go. She obliged.

February 1, 2004

Sunday. Woke up not feeling well, no parties for me today. Today is Super Bowl Sunday. We stayed home to watch it. I missed the Janet Jackson costume malfunction.

February 2, 2004

Monday. Woke up in pain; it is four AM Have major upset intestines. Went to the toilet, constipated again, stayed awake and laid down, kept trying to relieve this; this is the worst part of back surgery I think.

February 6th, 2004

Tuesday. I woke up and got dressed. Left leg is feeling bad; I mean real bad, pain down the shin to the foot. It's like its getting hit over and over with a hammer. Took pain meds and will call Dr. Schnitzer's office later to find out what is up. My pain is too high for me!

Getting stressed from the HMO and IDA people; Toni called from Dr. Schnitzer's to tell me she got the PMD referral. What a joke, five weeks after the first submittal! I had called IDA and Health Net to raise hell too. We must have been having ESP or something; Toni was very angry with them because I am in so much pain. These nerves are ripping my brain apart with pain and there is no stopping it, even with the strong narcotics I am on.

I got the referral faxed to me, and I called Dr. Abraham's office. I spoke to Jennifer; I asked for the soonest appointment, and she said Feb 23rd. I almost threw up! I took the appointment and told Jennifer to call me if another opens sooner; she said it's not likely. I called Toni back and left a message. I am very upset. I took my meds and a Valium.

I have never had so much pain and stress at once like this. It is like no one cares when a person is suffering. I ate lunch, and then took more meds. Cutting it close, but I need the extra strength and pain relief. I watched TV, and then fell asleep after taking another Valium.

February 7, 2004

Saturday. Woke up in intense pain, same as yesterday. The drugs finally knocked me out like the other day. I get numb and am asleep. I can hear sounds but I can't move. I took more meds and a Valium. I napped. It is one PM Bonnie got locked out. She woke me up to unlock the door. I told her I was so drugged I couldn't wake up; she had been knocking and calling for a long time. My pain is so terrible that it makes me lose thoughts and names. I worked on the diary.

Darla came home about 3 PM with the kids from a snow day.

I took more meds; the leg is burning now with pain from the nerves through the thigh to the foot. It spreads out like your skin is on fire and the nerves are dying and sending murderous pain sensations to the brain. This is getting to be endless. I ate dinner, fish and veggies. Leg is totally on fire with pain. Took full meds, watched TV, and fell asleep.

February 8, 2004

Sunday. Woke up, it is like ten AM I am so groggy, wow! I took three Norcos with the Vistaril. It was like a delayed-action shot; at first you feel a sensation of drugs like a morphine shot, but in a lighter way. Then the pain lessens, if at all. It doesn't go away completely, it just cuts the pain some. My leg has now been in constant pain, never stopping now. I just cut it with the drugs. When I take a larger dosage and knock myself out, then I can get rest. But this state of mind is not good.

Darla and I met to talk about noon. Our relationship has been bad. With the stress of the business debt and our partners having our lives in their control we are at a bad spot. Darla and I really had a row. The argument got terrible with the anger of the past and the present debt load. I know the company may not survive. My people are trying hard, but we cannot borrow more money.

If it crashes, then we lose everything. Darla has a tremendous fear of this. I have said maybe we should split up and sell the house. She would get her share. She is very angry that she has to pay my debts, as she calls them, for the business. We have reached a bad rut in our relationship.

I continue to take meds to help me, as I am stressed out now from this senseless argument. People have such small thoughts of only themselves. I guess this is the nature of our species, which is to survive through all the stresses, blame others.

I am resting now; it is about four PM I am trying to get

some pain-free time. My leg is so bad and now at times even the whole nerve from the hip/back to the foot is like it is burning with fire. This is so incredible. Worse than the first day when the disc exploded. I wonder if my disc has compressed and the nerve is getting hit again. Why should I have such great pain?

I finally slept after the stressful time, and when I awoke I wrote Darla a letter and emailed it to her. To let her know of my wrong decisions at times, yet, I only hoped for the best. If the business dies, which I don't think will happen, it has good people running it. It has a certain value; if sold, our stock is worth enough we could be debt free and keep our house. If we sold that we could live simpler and I could, I am sure, work again someday soon.

February 11, 2004

Wednesday. Woke up and got the documents together for Juan to pick up. I have selected a law firm to handle the action/claim against the rehab office and doctors. I am in such a bad way it is necessary to protect my family. Emailed some files to Jeff, the attorney. I typed in my diary. Need to take more meds; my leg is beyond pain.

February 12, 2004

Thursday. It is just past midnight. I am up writing in my diary. I have had a tough day, took lots of meds, and stayed in bed most of the day. The pain is increasing, I want to exercise and do more, but the pain is too much. I don't want to re-injure anything by exercising without having a professional work me through the proper things to do.

My nerve pain is increasing like there is compression again. I'm wondering if the vertebrae have slipped due to the lack of disc material for separation. All I know is I must take lots of meds to cope with this. My lifestyle is one of lying in bed for hours at a time, then a little activity until I must sit down or lay down, since sitting is such a killer on the back. Time to take more meds; the leg is throbbing after only fifteen minutes of sitting up.

February 13, 2004

Friday the 13th. I went with Darla to pick up the records we need from Emergency Hospital, Dr. Hanlon's, and our local hospital. We then went to Office Depot, copied everything, and purchased ink refills. Darla brought me home. I was exhausted, and my leg hurt horribly. I took three of each of my meds, laid down, and slept.

The kids are home from school; it is about 3 PM They woke me up so I took more meds; my leg is still throbbing. It is now about 4 PM, got a call from Toni at Dr. Schnitzer's office, and she said to call the IDA folks and raise more hell to get the approvals. I did. Toni called me close to 5 PM and we got the okay for the pain med doctor. She faxed the referral to me. I sent it to Dr. Abraham's office; we have a February 23rd appointment. I also worked on a pulmonary appointment. Wendy from the insurance company called and she said Toni would handle that, but it is also approved. Hoorah, we are getting there.

This caused so much stress. It is now 7 PM, and I took two Valiums to calm me down from all this phoning and going through routines with trained phone people trying to put you off. So I took more meds to settle in for the night, more Vicodin and Vistaril. Pain is still there, no change in the left leg, numbness is constant and now it is also hypersensitive to touch.

February 14, 2004

Saturday. The kids and Darla went to the snow for a Boy Scout snow day. It is Valentine's Day. I heard the kids have a good time with the cards and candy but I didn't get up until 2 PM I got up and called Darla; she said that Becky and Gary would be bringing the motor home over. They had offered to go to Irvine to get it from the broker who made the year/estimate mistake.

Gary brought it home and parked it in the space like I do. We are missing a set of keys; I am not happy about this. After they left I took three each of my meds. Needed to catch up on meds, too much pain.

Today I mostly rested. I am not feeling well mentally. I don't know what is wrong, it is hard to swallow and I get the hiccups a lot. I ate dinner with Darla. She checked out the motor home and commented on the missing keys. I hope we aren't being set up for a theft. We will keep our things out of it for a while. I am feeling more pain in the leg; these Vicodin just aren't cutting the pain. I took two more of each and Valium. Read and played with the kids a little, they had a nice time in the snow earlier today. I missed not being able to go …

February 15, 2004

Sunday. I woke up on the couch, really groggy. Left leg has 8 plus level pain on the inner side from the knee to the foot and wrapped around the ankle. Got up and ate. Drank water and took more meds. Watched the Daytona 500, not too highly interesting for me. I am not feeling good. My throat feels like something is stuck in it; I have had numerous hiccup episodes.

At lunch my left leg erupted in even greater pain! *What is up with this*? I took more meds. I have stayed in bed all morning, not moving other than to use the toilet or take a short shower. The pain in my throat is irritating.

I watched Dale Earnhart Jr. win the Daytona 500. What great excitement to accomplish a lifetime event like that. Even on the same day his late father won his only Daytona 500.

The kids came in and wanted some money for the ice cream man. I gave them $6 since they had some friends over too. The kids have been playing outside, which is good. It is now near 5 PM, I spoke to my mother on the phone, and everyone is well. We talked about Becky's friend Gary who came and got the motor home for us. What a fiasco that was. We have it back now, and I am okay with that. If we sell it, good, if not then we keep it, but the payments are scary while I'm not working and not making money.

I know I am an owner and deserve to be paid, but my partner has taken over and wants to cut my pay by 50% when I return to work so he can hire a new salesman. This is putting huge pressure on Darla and me as to what to do. We cannot continue long without any income, and then once I do go back to work it will be with a 50% cut in pay.

The company is struggling with low sales and production, and cash is tight. Darla and I don't have much left, and we are trying to refinance or take a line of credit on the house. But Darla and I cannot agree on what to do. This is a tough time for us.

I watched a movie on TBN on Paul of Tarsus, very well done. I had to take two more meds of everything. Is this 60 or 80mg, I am not sure, of codeine? My leg is in constant pain in all parts at various times. Sometimes the whole sciatic nerve is raging in pain like it is on fire with electricity, even with all these meds!

Last weekend I went off the meds to see if I could take it. And no way could I function. It is like the torture of the highest pain. My leg is weak and I tire easily, so I am staying low. At times I can't seem to even get to write in this diary.

February 23, 2004

My appointment with Dr. Abraham got changed to the 9th of March. It is okay, though, as I am not feeling well, getting stiff and swollen.

February 26, 2004

Went to have MRI's taken for my upcoming appointment with Dr. Schnitzer on Friday. This went smoothly for once. As this day progressed I tried to go to the toilet and nothing happened except that I started to experience great pain in my side like a kidney stone coming out. I really am in great pain and finally even after more meds and lying on my side I became incoherent. I told Darla we must get the hospital. I am in massive pain in my gut.

We go back to the hospital, and I am admitted. They give me DiLaudid, thank God for that, as I was delirious with pain and sinking into states of babbling and having difficulty breathing. They did an X-ray and found my colon impacted from a large stool. They checked my meds and found I was tripling the doses. They were upset and admitted me to the surgery wing and told me I either must pass this stool or have it taken out in a new surgery.

I am scared; as they won't give me more DiLaudid, they want me to pass this. They take me to the wing and the nurse goes to get the pump to pump me up to help evacuate this. I am on an IV, so I crank it up to full and begin drinking loads of water and another nurse brings me in some prune juice. I am so frightened of another wave of this horrible pain as I am passing out as it happens.

I am waiting for this nurse with the pump; she has been gone a long time. Darla went back home to be with the kids. I am alone. Finally, as I lay here in the hospital bed, I feel like my insides are blowing up. I get up and make it to the toilet, and *whoosh*, out goes this "thing." The nurse showed up right then with the pump, what timing. She looked at this thing and estimated it weighed ten pounds! She was right, as I had been weighed upon entry, and then we weighed again to check.

She said this is like having a big baby, and welcome to motherhood! I was so pooped, not a pun either! I was wiped out.

But I thanked God it was gone. The nurse checked the meds I was taking and told me that the Vicodin had caused this, and I should have been doubling my laxatives, which I wasn't. This is such a misery to endure, and I want it to end!

After a while the doctor came in and said all is well and discharged me to home. I called Darla, even though it was near midnight, and she came to get me.

February 27, 2004

Today is Friday, and I go to see Dr. Schnitzer at 9 AM I am exhausted, and Darla is too. She is getting to be a wreck with all the up and downs of my ordeal. Dr. Schnitzer says I cannot take the amount of codeine I am on, as the meds will damage my kidneys. He discusses putting me on morphine or heroin. I leave his office with Darla and tell her I am done with this crap and will take no more and tough this out. She takes me home and goes to work.

I have stopped all the meds cold turkey. I begin to convulse and shake and tremble. Bonnie, my oldest daughter, comes in and is holding me. Darla comes home and it is getting serious as I am violently shaking, crying, and getting weird visions of bugs, and all kinds of fearful things.

Darla and Bonnie are freaking out and want to call 911. I tell them I will deck the first paramedic through the door. I want no more meds and will get through this. I am on the couch in the living room, shaking uncontrollably with crying and emotions running wild. I am detoxing from the drugs, and this is horrible.

Darla runs outside to get help and coming up the street were a pair of LDS missionaries. She hails them and they come inside and begin to pray and hold me. Several men come in, neighbors I think, and hold me. I am shaking and throwing these guys around the couch with my uncontrollable shakes and crying. It is an awful time. This continues for hours.

There are moments when I am lucid, then it hits again with horrible shakes, emotions, and even sights of massive bugs on the walls creeping toward me. I am getting very tired. But it continues. Finally I settle down with no more shakes. After a time the men and LDS missionaries leave. Darla thanks them, and so do I. I am weak and still trembling but better. No 911, no more drugs.

February 28, 2004

No more drugs through the night, just crying and depressive bouts. All day this continues, crying and shakes. Through Sunday and into Monday I am lying in different rooms of the house just trembling and crying with melancholy. Darla keeps someone with me during this time as I think she is fearful of my doing something to myself. On Monday the same thing as I finally sleep in Hannah's room for hours, crying whenever I wake up. This continues but is getting better now. On Tuesday I make Darla stay home with me to comfort me. I am off the drugs and very weak and needful of love, comfort, and assurance. It is the first time we talk deeply of all that has happened. I am getting my mind back to the person I was just weeks ago.

March 4, 2004

On Thursday I made Darla stay home again, and we went to Covina where I grew up. I walked on the street where my parent's home is. Floods of memories came in during this very emotional time as I am shakily off the meds. I mean, I am taking nothing. But the pain is there. Now my back is the issue with a glass grinding pain right in the lumbar level after 20 minutes or so of being upright. It causes shooters down my left leg. But my mind is back, and I am willing this thing through. Being in Covina helped. I also visited my Father's gravesite. Needed to do that.

I am in pain, but beginning to deal with a method of no drugs to soothe the pain. A few minutes up, then an hour or two down, or use the inversion chair to unload the L4-L5 vertebrae that are grinding together. The leg is still bad.

March 9, 2004

At my appointment with the pain management doctor, he was aghast at my story and that I have kicked the meds myself. He has never seen this before. He approves water therapy and gives me an epidural shot right in the tailbone. He uses refrigerant to freeze the spot and, man, is it cold! But hey, I am driving now, and this is a boost to my spirits.

March 26, 2004

Friday the 26th. The first step of water therapy is an exam. The office is 10 miles from my house, and I am driving myself. Everyone is amazed but happy, me too. But the back is still a problem with this barely 20 minutes up and then the feeling of grinding broken glass in my spine with killer pain equivalent to a zillion hot knives piercing the nerves. The leg is calming down with waves of pain every few hours.

March 29, 2004

My first water therapy is today. It is hard to drive with all the bumps and transitions in the roads that just kill my back and legs. I get very exhausted and sweat in pain. But I am doing it. I do the first therapy and have to stop. The back is good in the pool, but the pressure on my leg is intolerable! This is a blow!

I am in tears, leaving in great pain, lying in the gym locker to recover from the pain so I can drive home.

I come home and notify Dr. Abraham and Dr. Schnitzer's office for instructions. They say to come in next month and to take it easy. So now it is a waiting game. I have been hoping to go back to work in a limited fashion in April. After kicking the meds and pushing past the pain, the hope was my body would heal and I could resume a life of sorts. So this is a blow to my hopes and puts added pressure on us financially; we are getting close to no return.

Life has been better for Darla and the kids with me off the drugs, as I would not take morphine or heroin in front of our small kids. I am so much better dealing with this the way I am now. But I am depressed again over the loss of healing to my body and the horrible shape I am getting in from no exercise and getting flabby.

My company has stabilized with all the inputs from the different sources. The moment of the disaster of my injury, and everyone reacting to it in different ways froze the place up and it cost a ton of money. With much input from staff and the partners it is rolling again. A week ago they agreed to pay a small offset for the use of my license to help us get through the time ahead. I borrowed against my stock and this will now pay that back and give us a little cash each week to keep afloat.

I managed to get our mortgage loan holder for the house to reduce the payment and we are cutting way back on all other costs to manage until I return to fulltime work. It has been a struggle and I pray that now the worst is over.

ARTIFICIAL DISC TECHNOLOGY

Late March, early April 2004

Now we are through for a time with the extraordinary series of events leading from the injury to my surgeries to my recovery and to the uncertain future of my spine and health. By late March, early April 2004, I had come to the place where I could function daily using various techniques to unload my spine through hanging upside down on an inversion table and chair and lying down for long periods to take the pain away. I was taking no medication. I was going in for periodic epidural shots from my pain management doctor to help with the leg and back pain.

My hopes were to return to work; I even had driven over to the office in late March to visit, but it was obvious I could not do this daily, or even once a week, as it took me two days to recover from the hard drive of one hour each way. Life was settling into a rhythm of my days of healing, appointments with doctors, and visits with friends and family. I was now working from home on the computer with my staff, and trying to do phone calls to stay on top of what I could.

As my neurosurgeon had suggested, I began to investigate the technology of artificial disc replacement surgery that had been developed in Germany in the early 1980's, leading to a device called the Charite SBIII by 2004. It was in clinical trials here in the USA but, according to Dr. Schnitzer, would not be approved for probably two more years. He felt I could wait that long.

We didn't know then about the grinding of the vertebrae due to the excised disc during surgery. This unfortunately hastened the timing of a decision. Thus begins the journey down the road to the making a choice between new versus old technology.

April 2004

In early April of 2004 I had resolved that I must make a decision to have a fourth surgery of either a spinal fusion at level L4-L5 or a somewhat new to USA technology using moving implants called artificial discs. Dr. Schnitzer had now restricted me to driving to appointments only and he ordered more studies of my spine to find the cause of the grinding.

He was concerned over the muscle damage to my left leg and the resultant failure of water therapy. He ordered massage therapy to loosen the knots in the muscles from the spasms I was having daily. This alone was a mystery, as at any time my left thigh or leg would just erupt in massive spasms with the muscles pumping like a locomotive.

The month of April was spent rethinking my path ahead, dealing with the fact I may have a long road ahead of recovery from one more surgery and all the unknowns that brings. I began the process of gathering the information needed to understand the spine and the options available to me to resolve my unique painful situation. Here is what I discovered.

In mid-April I began a series of short Internet sessions as I could only sit for about 30 minutes before my back gave out from the bones hitting. During these windows of time I found support groups on the boards with people who had been through all I had (well, not three back-to-back surgeries) but some had been through experiences that were horrible, worse even than mine. I began processing this information and started the research to discover insights into the ADR (artificial disc replacement) world.

Much to my wonder at this time there was next to nothing on the Internet about this type of surgery and technology. During one session I came across a posting from a man who had traveled to Germany the year before to have this ADR surgery! I posted to him and, amazingly, he was a local Southern California resident. I called him, and this is how I met Mark Mintzer, through our common journey through similar spine injuries.

Mark told me his story and how he had researched ADR technology early in 2002, and ultimately chose a small clinic in Munich to have his amazing two level lumbar Charite ADR surgery performed. Mark was incredibly informative. He had just decided to start a new business to be a liaison for back pain sufferers like himself to help them get access to the proper information, and to help them gain access to the spine doctors involved in bringing this amazing new surgery to the USA marketplace.

Mark and I spoke at great length about my situation and my options. He gathered that I could find this ADR information myself as it seemed to him that I was informed enough to do this myself, as he had the year before. He gave me a small cost estimate to have him digitize my films and send them to Germany, but I figured that with his input I could do it myself. After consulting over this with Darla and digesting the information about this new technology, Darla and I agreed it was worth investigating. I had a massage appointment the next day at the therapy office. I went to it and, to my amazement, my therapist told me she knew of a local doctor doing the ADR surgery in the clinical trial. I got his name, contacted his office, and received an appointment for early May! Was I stoked now!

A brief primer on ADR technology:

In the modern medical world of advanced surgical technology, it was only a matter of time before manmade science inventions would improve on the world of spinal fusion devices that had been used since the mid-1960's.

Technology is advanced as new materials are discovered and research is made into the applicability of these materials, especially in the human body where rejection of these materials is a serious factor. The device is placed within this precise and delicate structure involving the spine itself, the spinal cord, and the surrounding structure.

These challenges added to the slow development of this technology, due to the difficulty in diagnosing whether the source of pain is coming from the discs or the facet joints. This is the leading factor in the long-term research that is required to identify and test the design restrictions and the materials needed to engineer a proven motion-preserving and compatible device.

The end result is the goal of restoring near normal physiological function and to eliminate the patient's pain. As this technology was developed in a country free of restrictive government agencies, the device development became available in the early 1980's in Berlin, Germany. The actual hospital was the Charite University Hospital, renowned for its orthopedic advancements.

In the late 1980's the Charite SB ADR device was in an early stage of development and had been placed in the first hundreds of patients with limited success. With newer versions, by the late

1980's and early 1990's, this technology had become an option available only in European countries where no governmental agency approval was required.

By the late 1990's this device caught the attention of a major American corporation that purchased the Charite technology and then applied for the necessary FDA approval clinical trial process that I had come across by early 2004. By this time, of course, other companies had seen the light of this new advancement and had developed similar ADR devices that were also under FDA trial studies.

This became for me a truly fascinating education in the process of how companies, technology, and the marketplace interact into streamlining the final product that receives FDA approval and then dominates the American marketplace. However much I was intrigued, my back reminded me that a decision had to be made soon.

April 2004

Throughout April it was continual massage therapy, doctors' appointments, reading up on ADR and spinal fusion technology, and trying to survive each long painful day filled with frustrating pain and limited ability to move. At the same time I was trying to maintain a working relationship with my company, staff, and clients from home with a limited amount of time that I felt up to being on the phone or even seeing my staff at my home.

In early May I was anxious with anticipation to visit the first ADR doctor right here near my home. So on May 6th I went with Darla to visit Dr. Chandler, a spine surgeon, involved in the clinical trials using the Pro Disc device, a device to the similar Charite design.

This meeting was a stunner as Dr. Chandler announced to me that my spine was horribly unstable and the disc was ready to rupture again! He told me to stay home in bed and wait for 12 to 18 months for the device to be approved so he could do a two level implant, as my L3-L4 disc was also bad. I was stunned! He told me he wanted to do a nerve EMG test on my left leg to determine the amount of neurological damage. We set this up, but I left his office in tears.

The next day a friend had arranged for a home massage therapist to visit me and provide more massage therapy. I really needed this relaxing massage as I was shaken from the events of yesterday. Paul did a mild Shiatsu massage, neither of us knowing the reaction to come. Later that night I felt stiff and laid down, as Mother's Day was the next day and I wanted to feel well.

May 2, 2004

Mother's Day, I am sick, vomiting black stuff and the same is oozing out of my pores. I am in an awful way. It is hard to move. All day I am in the toilet heaving.

May 3, 2004

Illness continued into today. I had to cancel physical therapy. I am so sick, lethargic, and stiff.

May 4, 2004

Tuesday, I am better, much better, and have an appointment with Dr. Schnitzer. I tell him about the meeting with Dr. Chandler. He tells me this procedure is now appropriate for me and directs me to Cedars-Sinai Medical Center to see a Dr. Regan. I also tell him about the reaction to the massage. He explains that I must be careful about this. No more Shiatsu style as this released toxins from all the meds. But boy, I feel so much better! He agrees that in my case it probably has helped.

Back to more research on who Dr. Regan is and ADR technology. I call Cedars and set up an appointment with Dr. Regan for early June. He is doing the Charite ADR here! This is encouraging for me. As May progressed I got into more weekly physical therapy massages with the Tens unit electrical stimulation to ease my nerve pain. I began taking natural supplements to help with the toxin release. I was now in a routine of hanging upside down several times a day to relieve the bone grinding and pain. It even seemed to help my leg spasms and shooting pains.

Friends, co-workers, and family visits were the norm and I even made calls to a few close-by clients to help stimulate the juices of getting back to work. Thinking about the upcoming appointment with Dr. Regan and hoping for a new turnaround in this journey.

By mid-May I was now cycling on and off the daily rhythm of resting to ease the pain and taking a sleeping pill with an antidepressant. It seemed to help.

In late May I went to Dr. Chandler's office again for the EMG nerve test. This was quite painful as the test is one where electrical probes are inserted into the muscles and shocks are administered to the wires to stimulate the nerves. This required many insertions and a burning of the shin to get the result. The result of the test was nerve damage to L4 and L5 nerves in the left leg. Heck, I could have told them that.

June 2, 2004

Finally, the big day has arrived. My wife's birthday and the appointment scheduled with Dr. Regan at Cedars-Sinai. What anticipation again! We drove to Beverly Hills with my brother-in-law Dan. Once there and checked in, we waited as the physician's assistant came in and introduced herself as Dr. Lauren. She went over my case and was amazed at my ordeals and that I was not on meds. This was a new one for her.

In came Dr. Regan and I immediately knew he was excellent. He was truthful and honest. He reviewed my case and asked if the previous ADR doctor had ordered a disc-o-gram, a specialized X-ray, to find which discs were generating the pain. He stated that without this test it is impossible to say that a two-level ADR surgery would be required.

He examined me and thought that if a disc-o-gram showed negative for the L3-L4 he would perform surgery on me in the clinical trial using the Charite implant as a one-level approved candidate. Wow, was I impressed. We then proceeded to fill out the application for surgery and set up the disc-o-gram test. Dr. Regan answered the many questions I posed, even telling me about his problems with placements and the subsequent nonsuccessful results. These were honest replies to my queries into a new technology where there has been little true patient feedback here in the USA.

After we completed the application Dr. Regan came back and showed us the device model. I was impressed with his care and thoughtfulness to do that. We left and I was on cloud nine, so hopeful about having this operation.

Once home, calls came in immediately from Cedars-Sinai's Surgery Department setting up the surgery for a couple of weeks from now and the disc-o-gram test for a week before that. Then trouble, a call came in from Dr. Regan's nurse saying my insurance would not authorize the non-network provider coverage for this test. I was stupefied. Then, realizing this, I called Toni at Dr. Schnitzer's for help. She jumped through the hoops and got an approval for a local in-network disc-o-gram.

So far so good, then the unhitching occurred. Michelle called from Cedars-Sinai Hospital Scheduling Department to advise that my insurance would not be accepted due to the fact that Cedars is out of network. Again I was incredulous, to be this close to this type of surgery and then to find out there is no coverage! Back on the phone for another round of calls, then the truth, not only is there no coverage, but that the clinical trial is not covered nor is subsequent care. For an FDA-approved trial! You have got to be kidding me!

Only months later when a case manager was assigned to me, was this revealed to be bogus information. But by then it was too late and I had already made my fateful decision. But at this time I was devastated that here I was so close and now it was all a new loss on my emotional rollercoaster. Boy, was I hitting the anti-depressant pills hard now. I contact Dr. Regan's office to get a cash price for the surgery and am shocked at the estimate; it is almost enough to have purchased my home!

This is not going to work out. We are in no financial position to afford that high a medical expense. Darla is now telling me to give up on this and look into waiting or, if the ADR technology is not going to happen, to have a spinal fusion surgery performed by Dr. Schnitzer who has offered it to me. I am in a state of emotional distress trying to understand all the politics of medical-managed care, governmental policies, and my options.

June 2004

Going into mid-June I am in a state of mind where I want the ADR technology but I am under stress to return to work but I also need a surgery to somehow correct the missing disc in my spine and restore the vertebrae to a fixed position of proper height. Those nerves are getting whacked daily and I don't know how much more of this I can take.

Dr. Schnitzer thought I would last up to two years and it has only been five months since the surgeries. Already I am again in a vicious cycle of out-of-control pain and limited ability to function. Let alone the fact that every aspect of my life is hinging on this decision: the impact to my marriage, my family, my business, and my future.

I do the one thing I started earlier; I went back online to research the German hospitals and maybe contact them for an opinion as Mark Mintzer had suggested. I could see he was a great success from his testimony on the website for his new fledgling business of directing people to go to Germany. He was back to skiing, parachuting, flying, even playing soccer. So it seemed to me that the ADR solution was the best I could find because of the negative feedback I had now gotten from so many sources about failed spinal fusions.

Even Dr. Schnitzer seemed hesitant to perform a fusion on me. He indicated that due to my former great conditioning and age I was not a good choice for a fusion. I could decide to have it done but he was inclined toward the ADR industry as the ultimate choice. His preference was for me to wait it out. I was pushing to have this done, as I knew my time was limited by my goal to return to work to restore my family's financial future.

Mid-June, 2004

After a few days to recover from the insurance rejection and the out-of-sight cost of cash surgery at Cedars-Sinai's, I again searched the web pages and found a hospital in Bremen, Germany called Stenum Hospital that was a major Charite ADR surgery center. They had already performed over 600 Charite ADR implants with great success. Additionally they specialized in American cases to the point of having a complete package for travel, hotel, and hospital arrangements. All for a sum that was a fraction of the cost here in the USA. So, it's on to the next part of my journey, Germany.

After cascading through this series of events with doctors, clinical trials, and attempted insurance approvals, I ended up with only dismal rejections and disappointments. Incredibly I came across, on my own, this amazing web page with positive information, page upon page of glowing beautiful sights, and surgical reviews. There were also testimonies written by Americans who'd had incredible successes over the last eighteen months. All of them with an amazingly low incident rate of failure or re-surgery or problems with failed back surgery. Consequently, after digesting this new resource and even contacting some of the former patients who had traveled to Stenum Hospital in Northern Germany, I began the process to contact this hospital and make this a potential choice for my ADR option.

Late June 2004

After a frustrating session with another round of doctors and shots to help my pain, and with a shrinking list of options available here in the USA on the horizon, I got up late one night, pulled out the overseas phone card and dialed the number on the web page. To my surprise a pleasant sounding male voice, speaking excellent English, answered. I introduced myself to Mr. Petersen, the Stenum International Diplomat, who carefully listened to the story of my multiple surgeries and frustration with the American system of managed health care.

He was very familiar with all of this and we went into a detailed forty-five minute discussion of my spine symptoms. He requested I send him my films via FedEx. I thanked him for this incredible breath of fresh insight and amazing discussion with a representative of a hospital that was doing ADR surgeries weekly! He was so informative and knowledgeable. I was impressed and later that day, took the first actions to send my films via FedEx for the surgeon to review my case.

I did this within a couple of days and then waited. In less than a week an email arrived with the diagnosis of my case including the option and approval for a Charite ADR surgery at my L4-L5 level. They would make a closer examination of the L3-L4 level once I was in Germany to make a final determination of whether I should have a two level implantation. Also consideration was given to the fact that with continued waiting for surgery my spine would, with the L4-L5 disc removed, incur permanent facet joint damage that could lead to other issues that couldn't be addressed by ADR surgery.

With this report and information, it was decision time. Now another hard part was ahead, getting Darla, my wife, to agree to this surgery and the fact that it would not be covered by our insurance. We would have to pay cash for it with money we didn't have, unless we used our line of equity from our house.

During late June and early July, as I digested this and we discussed our options, it was clear that Darla was not for it. She thought the fusion surgery would be better. Maybe I wouldn't be as mobile, she admitted, but with the potential problems of going overseas it was too much for her to take on. Plus the fact that the surgery here was covered for the most part and that the German ADR surgery would be a huge cost to us financially.

During these trying days of testing my self-will and her position, things were very tense. I had all but decided this was the best solution for me. Being married, though, brings the need for a compromising aspect to these types of decisions. After many nights of discussions and enduring long days of being in a quandary as to what I should do, I finally snapped at her and demanded the money to go with her or without her.

She was not amused. But she could see that after days of struggling internally, I was internally ready to do what I had to do. It was an emotionally tough moment for both of us. Her security versus my health, two very diametrically opposed positions. After this stand off, Darla agreed, but with the stipulation that whatever happened this would be it. Any failure would have to be redone in the USA by the established medical group we belonged to. I couldn't agree fast enough.

All the time we were in a period of extreme tension due to our tenacious financial situation and, of course, the pressure of the company debt hanging over us while we had little input into the course the company was going. Add this to all we had previously been through and now with the uncertain aspect of more surgery in a foreign land, well...you get the picture.

The next obstacle to overcome was getting banking approval for refinancing our home for an equity line of credit. Meeting with an estate attorney to set up a trust for our family and writing a will in case something happens to us in flight, all the thousand and one details. Doctor appointments here for pre-surgery checkups and then transferring the reports to Stenum Hospital.

Through all this time of busyness, stress, and wonderment over these events, I am also dealing emotionally with the fact that each day I am potentially causing more irrevocable damage to my spinal nerves and tissues. So as we approach the time for the flight over to Germany, I am taking more sleeping pills and really pouring massive amounts of natural supplements into my body.

However, on the other hand, I am elated for this incredible opportunity. It was possible that I could return from Germany in late August and be back at work and have complete recovery by October. This would be the fulfillment of the hopes that these many months of pain and suffering were going to become just a memory; that I was finally on the road to the medical end of this journey.

July 31, 2004

As the tension of this momentous event drew near, on July 31st, tension between Darla and I hit another bursting point of differing emotions. We had a major argument over money primarily, with the stress of the business debt the secondary point. With all these stresses and my continued poor physical state, plus her being overloaded with the stress of the kids, the house, her time off to go with me, maybe losing her job as a result, this was a serious overload that was like a Santa Ana wind coming in on a dry day. It lit off.

No need to go further, other than that night I popped a few Vicodin and Valium to offset the highly agitated state of emotions that had triggered more pain in me. She may have taken a Valium too; she certainly deserved one. Dr. Schnitzer called them happy pills.

GERMANY

──•◦•──

August 3, 2004

The day arrives. We ride out to LAX and go through check in and settle in on the plane for our flight to Germany, a long thirteen hours for someone in the shape I am in. Post three surgeries, nerves inflamed, pain streaking everywhere, and filled with nervous anticipation for this eventful, momentous trip.

Darla and I are doing okay, but we are nervous, stressed, and worried for our kids during this big trip together considering all the uncertainty surrounding the last nine months of our lives. So we say a little prayer as we take off and wish each other well. We arrive in Germany after long flights, first to the airport in Amsterdam, and then on to Bremen.

We are exhausted and nervous. We are picked up and driven to a wonderfully beautiful hotel, just a block from the hospital, a truly magnificent place in Saxony, Germany. We rest, take in the sights of the area, and begin the jet de-lagging.

August 5, 2004

Yesterday we were processed—well, I was, into the hospital. After a long tedious day of checking in, more tests, waiting, seeing all the people from the States here for the same surgery, finally late in the evening, I am admitted. Met the doctors, Mr. Petersen, and other Stenum officials. So much going on it is exhausting. But like any major event it is filled with adrenaline as the time draws near.

My surgery is set up for the seventh at nine AM I spent the day of the sixth in the hospital preparing by taking certain concoctions the doctors and nurses prepared to clear me out and had the final pre-surgery tests. I am seeing the returning post-ADR surgery patients being brought to the American wing, as they call it. The hospital is under construction to expand due to the constant flow of Americans coming over for this surgery, actually from all over the world.

We are meeting those who are also assigned to our room (three to a room for the men) and their families. It is good for Darla and the spouses to have these other family members here during this time of waiting for loved ones to return after surgery. It is somewhat overwhelming to think that they schedule ten to fifteen a week. It does cause the nurses here, who struggle with English, difficulty in their efforts to accommodate the very different Americans who desire things to be just like back home.

It certainly isn't like home here. First, of course, there is the language, but also the signs, light switches, doors, bedding, power receptacles, food, medications, nursing, jokes, the heating and air conditioning system (there is no AC, heating only) and it is very hot for this part of Germany. The bees are everywhere in the hospital, stinging us in our beds; yes, even in our rooms.

For sensitive Americans it was quite a time, especially for those of us confined to beds after radical surgery. Finally my time arrived and, after all these months of waiting for my next surgery, it is now. I am glad, yet scared about the result, praying for success. The surgeons examined me yesterday and without much ado stated my L3-L4 disc was compromised and must be removed. So a two-level implantation was approved and we had to wire over more funds to pay for it.

SUCCESS AND DISASTER AGAIN

———❖———

August 7, 2004   **Surgery #**4

Into the surgery room for my Charite ADR surgery, it is now time to undergo a radical, scary, yet seemingly commonplace, for here anyway, surgery. Now all the waiting was over, and I was wheeled into the operating room, and the time had come.

Seemingly I was out only for seconds, even though it was actually over two hours. They told me later that it was one of the longer implantation surgeries. I awoke in the recovery room with a spinal catheter readied with a morphine pump for when the anesthesia wears off. The nurse asks your pain level and the pump is activated and set to drip morphine directly into the surgical area.

You are kept in this room twenty-four hours for recovery and then brought back to your room for complete recovery. Once I awoke they asked my pain level and, to my surprise, I had none. I mean *no* pain. A slight pain to my abdomen where the incision was as the approach to the spine for the ADR implantation is made ventrally or through the anterior angle of the body to the spine. But, compared to the previous back surgeries, this felt more like I was just doped up from the anesthesia.

Therefore no morphine was given and, indeed, they removed the catheter after some discussion with the doctors who were amazed that I needed no morphine. Of course, I had for weeks prior to this surgery been taking massive amounts of a supplemental oxygen mineral liquid recommended by a therapist. I believe this was the reason for the greatly reduced pain level.

I felt so good, I was able to get up in recovery less than two hours after surgery, another surprise to the German medical staff at Stenum Hospital. In fact I insisted on walking to use the bathroom instead of using the catheter placed *you know where*. They had a fit over this, but I won out as the doctors came in, looked me over, and were amazed at my incredible condition.

I took a short walk down the hall with a walker and a nurse, and *viola*, a *piece de résistance*, as they say in France. Then instead of a day in the recovery room, they agreed to let me go back to my room where one of the Americans was telling my room companions how he had just seen me walking down the hallway. They did not believe him. Then minutes later I walked in with my nurse. My room companions were in shock, as well as were the spouses and family members.

All true and verified. I was back in my room and within a day I was walking everywhere. I was so stoked; this was my Mt. Everest achievement! It was the success I was hoping for, and everyone I could think of to call or tell was stunned at how great I was doing so soon after surgery. Certainly the surgeons were very amazed, even going so far as to say no German patient had ever achieved this incredible recovery without any morphine. They told us that Americans were so drug dependent that we came over with bottles of drugs and were hard to treat due to our sensitive systems.

Then I came and bounced through this difficult surgery. There was a newfound respect for Americans after that.

I was so happy to be pain free that I didn't care what anyone thought. I followed the recovery process in the room and took all the medications they gave me for the stomach movement, and all the orals and IV's for surgical recovery. It was just the quick exit from the recovery room that got everyone jumpy. I was just so impressed with this surgery! My left leg was almost pain free and I felt *taller*! Yes, taller indeed, as I had lost over one and a half inches from the disc removal. With a two-level implantation I was now close to two inches taller than a day before, an amazing occurrence. Of course I do not recommend this to anyone who wishes for height implants; this is definitely not the preferred method.

As each day progressed the functions of my body were restored. Yes, getting the bladder, kidneys, and stomach to return to functioning is a sweat-filled tense time. Naturally my colon was back to its usual post-surgery non-functioning with all the associated pains. But overall things were good. Getting to know two other American men and their families made it better. It was enjoyable to share stories and getting to know someone made a situation like this more tolerable.

Fred Korte from Arizona was a blast, and I can't mention all the exact things he did, but one time he took his morphine pump into the bathroom and gave it a big squeeze to blast away the pain. Boy, was Nurse Ralph amazed at the big, and I mean big, drop in his pump vial from only minutes before. Ralph was so confused and mumbling. That event was worth a daily laugh for all of us.

I was progressing fine, except that my abdomen was swollen more than the other guys, and was really red and bloody. At the time no one seemed to think it was significant. In a day or two, actually on Tuesday, I was released to the hotel, days ahead of schedule. It was a relief to be in the hotel where there was air conditioning and no more bees. But now I was suffering from the abdomen being so swollen. Then it happened, the first inkling of a problem. As I sat down to a meal in the hotel restaurant a sharp pain drove through my back above the lumbar level and put me onto the floor, under the table. Boy, did everyone scatter and did waiters run to help! I got up and slowly sat down, not knowing what had happened. I had heard of these "distraction pains" post-surgery, but that was a humdinger.

No one I had spoken with had experienced anything like that. Indeed, some men and women were dressing regularly in pants and back to normal within four to five days post-op. Here I was now five days, and I had a scare. Then it happened again and again, each time the same thing; a severe pain to my back and down I went. Back to Stenum Hospital for a check-up and an X-ray, tests for what were supposed to be for my release to go home.

The X-ray showed my L3-L4 implant had shifted into the center of the vertebrae, sinking upward into the cancellous bone material of the vertebrae. This symptom was called subsidence. The surgeons looked this over and expressed that it was irrelevant and would go away. I asked how long and they shrugged their shoulders with a look of insignificance. When I asked about my swollen stomach and its pain, they again said it was common to have some edema post-op.

So they approved my return home and without other input Darla and I left. Well, we actually went to visit some friends in a nearby town, the Idhe's, a close family we had come to love as our own. Their oldest daughter Nadine had stayed with us for six months as an exchange student. We used this opportunity to visit them, even in my condition of recovery. I needed rest and their home was a wonderful place to achieve this as it was nestled in a beautiful part of Germany.

After a week of comfort and renewing our friendships, a very good time for Darla and me, we bid our goodbyes and left for the states. During the flight home I was examined by doctors on the flight who pronounced that upon arrival in LA, Darla was to take me straight to a local hospital. This was due to the fact that I was becoming ill and the swollen abdomen was increasing in size with an obvious condition called a seroma. A dangerous leakage of fluids was building up in the abdominal cavity and putting pressure on my internal organs.

So, once again, we went from a frying pan into the fire with more problems and continued hospitalizations.

The day we touch down in Los Angeles, after two weeks spent in Germany and revolutionary surgery to perform ADR implants, I am back in the hospital where the first surgeries had taken place. As I have had a foreign country medical intervention with very foreign implants in my body you can well imagine the response of the doctors on staff that day. Here I am, wheeled in with agonizing pain to my abdomen, with my stomach protruding like an eight-month-term pregnant female, only I am not pregnant and am covered in surgical stitches. It was obvious I had something serious happening.

Thank goodness we'd had the foresight to include Dr. Schnitzer on all the plans and details, so upon landing he was contacted. At the hospital the admitting doctor refused to treat me due to the foreign object in me and who knew what else. Dr. Schnitzer arrived and demanded that my care be immediate and swift. And it was.

First, I was off to radiology for X-rays and tests. Then a call was made to pull in the ultrasound radiologist to perform a seroma evacuation of the serum built up in my abdomen. This was a delicate procedure, not without its own trauma, as over 950 mL of fluid was removed. A painful process of having a large straw-sized tube inserted into your abdomen, with an even larger puncture-type knife punched through your abdomen as you watch from the table.

Then more X-rays and consultations with doctors as the implants are quite unique and obviously the L3-L4 is sinking badly. After three days stay at the hospital, I came home, only to return for another round of the same once the seroma came back and more fluid removal. All in all a nice ten-day addition to my now pushing sixty days in hospitals in two countries.

Finally home and the reality sets in that all my best-laid hopes are now crushed in a darkening shrinking place where there are no good options and it is obvious another surgery is looming. After a week of recovery at home, I began the process to evaluate my situation with the new films, going to see first Dr. Schnitzer who sent me to see Dr. Regan, and to inquire of the De Puy Spine Company as to my rights as a failed Charite patient.

Dr. Regan examined me and was quite taken aback by the obvious size difference in the L3-L4 and L4-L5 implants, stating it appeared the wrong size was used, a too small set of implants for that level. He then made a call and sent a letter to the FDA to gain emergency approval to remove the implants and fuse me. This plea for help and his obvious stance of concern was comforting. He indicated this would take time, perhaps up to two months to get approval as the government is slow. He then advised me that without this immediate approval I would or could go past his safety zone of re-operation to my abdomen to approach the vascular wall and to get past all the scar tissue. A serious problem that had a time limitation imposed.

I then sought the De Puy Spine and FDA process for remediation efforts, all the while feeling a sinking feeling that I was doomed. During this time it was provident that Mark Mintzer interceded with his help and resources. He offered to get another German surgical diagnosis from skilled ADR specialists I didn't know. So I went this route and received news of the difficulties but that if I was to return to Germany they could (these other surgeons) perform surgery to remove the sinking implant and either fuse or put in a differing style of implant.

September 2004

I digested this new twist and continued to seek help from De Puy Spine and hoped that Dr. Regan could get approval from the FDA in time. As time marched on into September I made contact with De Puy Spine, the American company who owned and manufactured the Charite implant, for assistance. All the while I am getting worse with daily, hourly pain shocks to my back driving me to the floor.

In September I made contact with De Puy and without any delays a top official responded with a thorough review of my case and he made inquires to Stenum. As my emails and calls had been responded to as it was irrelevant. Then Dr. Regan contacted me in late September to advise me that no approval had come in from the FDA and now the time was past for him to safely operate.

Now I was truly on my own. Wondering what is going to occur next hoping for a solution. Still seeking the answer from modern medical science technology.

BACK TO GERMANY

Finally, after weeks of waiting, De Puy Spine responded that Stenum would take me back. Stenum then contacted me to advise me of the change in relevance to my sinking implant and that they would arrange for a trip back at their cost and a revision surgery to remove and then re-implant a correct size Charite implant. They admitted that a smaller size had been mistakenly used.

Mid-October, 2004

Plans were hastily made for my return for surgery set for October 23rd. Exactly ten months to the day from my first surgery, this being number five!

Since my wife Darla was not able to go with me due to so much time lost from her employment, I was faced with traveling alone. So I invited Mark Mintzer to go with me as a medical consultant. I mentioned before that he is a former ADR patient who was now helping people through his new business called Global Patient Network, a web-based business to advocate for those people who much needed a liaison to cut through the bottlenecks of doctors' schedules and insurance hoops. He would even at times drive patients to their appointments and discuss key aspects of surgery options with the doctors.

I had actually wanted my neurosurgeon, Dr. Schnitzer, to go with me for my first surgery in Germany. He had at first agreed, then had to decline due to his schedule. I was really relieved that a person like Mark was willing to go with me. I asked Stenum Hospital if he could not only come but would they allow him in the surgery as an observer? They agreed.

Late October 2004

I made a contract with Mark and invited him to accompany me at my expense. In late October we flew over to Germany to Stenum Hospital for a very unprecedented revision ADR surgery to remove a failed implant and re-implant a larger size almost three months after the first surgery. A highly risky radical surgery, yet I felt I had no choice as I was determined to have a working set of ADR implants.

Upon our arrival the surgeons again went over the high risks of this surgery and the plan for the revision. They informed me that they had only performed five revisions in all the previous ADR surgeries and this was the first re-implantation attempt. If re-implantation were not successful a fusion would be done. A fusion was a definite option for a failed ADR surgery as it is easier to make this correction.

TWO WEEKS OF HELL

We, meaning Mark and I, met with the surgeons and went over the need for a vascular certified surgeon to be present during this surgery to assist with the approach. We were informed the chief surgeon was vascular trained. We never received proof of this as in a certificate. In the USA a certified vascular surgeon is there for these types of high-risk surgeries.

Onto the preparation for my revision surgery, I again went through the process of the pre-surgery preparations. I was not alone. One of the females of the group in August had returned to have an additional posterior surgical fusion performed as her implants had become unstable. A persistently bothered feeling kept Carmen and I discussing the obvious question of what and how this had happened to both of us.

I was first in, scheduled for 9:00 AM and her surgery was set to follow when mine was completed. I went into the hospital the night of the 22nd and got ready.

October 23, 2004   Surgery #5

Early on the morning of the 23rd I made my calls to home and had a short time to talk to Mark and Carmen who had come over to see me prior to my surgery. Mark, of course, was getting prepped to observe this radical second ADR surgery.

At 9 AM I was wheeled into the same surgery room as in August. Getting too familiar with surgery rooms over and over it seemed. Surgery number five was now set to begin. I was moved onto the special ADR operating table, said a joke or two, and was out.

Once I awoke in the recovery room I was really spaced out and groggy. Seeing people around but not able to focus on anyone until I started to clear the fog in my head. This time I was clearly on morphine, no waiting as this was a major surgery, and I felt pain all through my body. I came to and spoke to the nurse in recovery. She came over to the bed, and I asked her to touch my leg; I couldn't feel anything!

Knowing I was on a morphine drip to the spine, I asked for it to be shut off. She refused; I asked again and again until finally she called the surgeon. It was now about five PM I found out I had been in surgery over six hours! So the morphine was important, I guess. But I wanted to feel my left leg to see if this surgery was successful in stopping the pain. Finally my request was granted by about six PM

It took two or three hours for the morphine to subside then I felt pain, pain that is unconscionable to bear. I still had no feeling in my left leg. Mark came in right then, only Mark. He looked like a doctor in his medical garb. I asked him to touch my leg and he responded that it was ice cold. He called the nurse; she checked it too. She then tried to find a pulse and she immediately called the surgeons. They tried too. No pulse in my left leg. I was then told I had to be taken to another hospital for testing. An ambulance was called, and I was transported, just hours after a major surgery, to the Red Cross Hospital in Bremen.

A CT scan was made of my left leg. The findings were that my left iliac artery from the aorta had closed down. A section over 7 cm had occluded from the long surgery and the retractor tool placed to move the artery.

I found all this out later. Then, I was in no shape to know what was going on. Mark was with all the doctors. The vascular surgeon at the Red Cross told him that this was very serious and that I had maybe a 25% chance of keeping my left leg. A bad situation!

I was taken back to Stenum to recover for a week since I was so recently out of surgery and in agonizing pain. The transporting in the ambulance, the CT, all the lying in different hospitals with absolutely no pain meds, was something no one deserves. Plus an incident happened during transport where we went to the wrong hospital and the paramedics forgot to set the gurney wheel locks. When they pulled the gurney with me on it unconscious, the gurney slammed to the pavement. Mark told me later he had never heard such an inhuman scream come from an unconscious person. We had gone from hope to hell. I was now in hell and torture for the next two weeks that I thought would never end.

Back at Stenum Hospital, I was placed in my room where the nightmare of tortuous pain continued, nothing I had experienced to this moment compared with this. On a scale of zero to ten, a thousand is the closest this could be. By now I have had five surgeries, and my body has built a tolerance to high-powered meds. As the first night of this torture went on, I was racked hourly with surges of pain through my back, my left leg, and my left side.

Nothing the nurses or doctors on staff did or could do stopped this hell of wave after wave of pain. I screamed in bloody torture to my Creator that He would please let this pass. Each wave would end only to start again hour after hour. The nurses ran to my aid as I hit the call button repeatedly to get more morphine shots or pills or to have a comforting human touch. It was obvious something bad had happened.

The nurses would come in and cry as they held me to try and soothe me. Doctors would wheel me into X-ray over and over to see if the implants had dislodged into my spinal cord. There were blessed moments of pain breaks of minutes, then an hour, and then back again to another wave of the most hideous pain a being could endure and still live. Every aspect of my brain was screaming in a tortuous cry as the nerves let go with the signals of extreme damage and electrical blasts to the brain.

I was no longer a man. I was only a connected sensory mechanism to a system of bundles of sensors that had been violated and were in anarchy to the host. Continuous waves of pain stripped every aspect of humanity from me as the next wave took me to another place of torture. This must be what hell is like where Satan's demons are waiting to condemn and torture those victims of their own lusts.

I didn't deserve this. I didn't hurt anyone. I shouldn't be here with this happening. Those were my lucid thoughts as this nightmare began and went and went on and on each day. Only people brought me some solace. As the day would break and the sun would glimmer and I would hear people, I would come up out of the waves of endless pain shocks to a moment of lucidity.

Mark had to leave on Tuesday for the States. He didn't wish to go considering my state and the awful things he knew that I didn't know then. Carmen's surgery had been postponed due to the extensive time it took to perform my revision. In fact, all the surgeries that day after mine were cancelled. It took all that the surgeons had to perform my radical surgery. So Carmen was able to stay with me during the day and keep me sane after Mark had to leave for a seminar in Chicago.

I called my wife and asked her to come over to take me home as I wished to die close to my family. I knew that this was the end of my life, as I could not go through much more of these endless nights of wave after wave of pain. Three times during that week I was rushed to ICU for pain strokes, which is breakaway pain that cannot be relieved by the prescribed medications. Your brain starts to hyper-react, causing your heart rate to skyrocket and your blood pressure to increase to dangerous levels, which can then lead to convulsions and a potential for a stroke or heart attack.

October 29, 2004

Darla arrived on Sunday the 29th. She came in to see me and we sat. I got up to walk and then sat down again, instantly tired. As she stepped out, I passed out. She came back to see me being rushed to ICU again. This time I had OD'd from the doubling and tripling of morphine injections for the pain waves. In ICU they wouldn't let Darla in. I was convulsing as I swam in and out of delirium.

All I remember was white-suited people, then my blood was on fire, and I thrashed in the bed screaming to let be out. My blood was burning inside my body and in my brain. I was going mad and dying at the same time. My wife was seeing her husband die a tortuous death or going through the hell of torture few wives have had to witness. They wouldn't let her in to see me in this state of delirious mind.

Slowly the antidote, after several injections, took hold and I was released from the chemically induced bondage. I collapsed in the bed in ICU to a stupor of sleep and slumber. My wife was allowed in and she stroked my hair as I lay in this hospital room thousands of miles from home. Only the two of us to endure this new passage through a door reserved for death, pain, and suffering that few go through. Why? How? Is it important to know when the path of your life becomes one of torment? All I knew was I was beaten, but my body wouldn't let go. My mind was completely broken from the endless torture of these shocks to my system, endlessly sucking the life that had once burned bright.

My wife wasn't prepared to witness the inhuman pain that I was experiencing. Pain that changed me from a fairly healthy man to a man now broken, weeping, and babbling. A man suffering abject fear of another wave of torture coming to attack endlessly the receptors in the brain that were receiving continuing signals of pain. Pain at the highest level a man is able to endure and stay alive.

If I could have, I am sure in my lucid moments, just prior to another wave of pain hitting, I would have taken measures to end my life, as what is the purpose of going through all of this? Instead of being relieved from suffering, my pain is simply escalating beyond the wildest imagination of torture. I was nothing, nothing of use at all, only endlessly waiting for the next attack. That is what I had succumbed to.

November 3, 2004

As these days passed through hour after hour of sheer agonizing time, the next passage was back to the Red Cross Hospital for a catheter angiogram procedure to open the closed left iliac artery. Dr. Paetz, a vascular surgeon at the Red Cross Hospital, arranged this procedure. I was transported to that hospital and taken to the angiogram radiological room.

I was prepped and taken off meds so my heart would stay strong during this procedure. I went in hoping and praying that it would be simple. I was placed on the hard table and as I lay on my back I immediately went into a new pain wave. I was no longer on meds of any type, other than Tylenol, per the vascular surgeon orders for this type of procedure.

The angiogram doctor approached me and, after a local injection to numb my right femoral artery, took a surgical blade to cut open my flesh and I jumped at the pain. She stopped and asked if I could actually feel that? I said very much so. Because of my reaction she gave me a second local injection. She waited and tried again, but the response was the same, I jumped. She was stunned and gave me one more shot. This time she said she could not give me any more shots. She cut and I gritted my teeth since it felt comparable to white-hot steel coursing through my leg.

Then I felt pressure and the test started with a burning sensation as the iodine coursed through my arteries. They told me it would take about fifteen minutes once I was on the table. After many sessions of the iodine and burning feeling, I was going insane with pain in my back, leg, and side. I finally couldn't take it and asked them to stop. Dr. Paetz came up and told me they had made ten attempts to open the closure with metal stents. All had failed.

He explained that they could try one more time and this time they wanted to go through my arm to my heart and through the left leg (they had moved over there after the first pass and made the same knife cut on the left side) at the same time. I told him I was in unspeakable pain partly because he had told me prior to this procedure that I could not move an inch. I told him it had already taken so long that I must stand up, or I would go insane.

He agreed to stop. He said one more attempt might damage my kidneys with the dye anyway. He stated he would proceed to close me up. This took a long time. Afterward they taped my groin with pressure tape and twenty pound bags of sand in order to seal the femoral arteries that they'd had to cut open on each leg to run the catheter through. They pressed very hard on the bags for fifteen minutes and then placed me on a new bed. Dr. Paetz looked at me sorrowfully and said, "I am sorry but now you must remain in this position for sixteen hours."

I moaned and asked, "How long have I been in this room?"

He replied, "Two and a half hours."

So much for a fifteen-minute procedure! I was in extreme pain and I had not been told that no meds would be given. And now to find out that I wasn't to move my body and I was to stay on my back? Oh, my God, this was horror, to not be able to move for sixteen more hours? My God, who could have thought this would be required?

Yet it was the truth, and the only reality I now faced was the fact that there was no way out of this situation, and right now I had to deal with this new extreme hardship. Off we were whisked to our room upstairs where the next phase of this hell would begin. Once there I was lifted gently onto the bed and set in place. The nurses then reminded me that I could not turn or rise up at all, that I must stay flat on my back until the next day at six AM It was now just two PM November 3rd. A day and night I will never in my life forget.

Before we even got to the Red Cross Hospital, I had insisted that Darla be allowed to spend the night in the room with me. It cost us sixty Euro, about eighty dollars US. I didn't want her to leave me alone after the procedure. I had feared another failure but little did I know what it meant to have a multiple catheter angiogram performed so closely after major back surgery. This was far beyond my worst nightmare.

We are in the room now for this duration of time to allow my open femoral arteries to close. I cannot move right or left or sit up. All the time I am in horrible pain from all of this and am only allowed to take Tylenol. Who could have conceived this new exacting form of torture? The Middle Age people who were subjected to the rack and other forms of torture to make them admit guilt sure missed out on this one!

As this day wore on, Darla was my solace and life. She kept me from more insane mental activity as she comforted me with cool compresses and made this time passable. She was my angel of love. I was in such agonizing pain as these hours wore on. Just being able to talk to her and have her with me in spite of our strained relationship from this entire ordeal and the prospect of her potentially losing her job for so much lost time. She had flown over in response to my emergency request. Now was the moment that I really needed her and she was here for me.

She rolled blankets and stuffed them under my sides to lift my back from the bed. The pressure from the bed to my damaged spine was so intense. She also used pillows to keep my head up a bit, and whenever the nurses came in she would ask for help to keep me as comfortable as possible.

Finally as the evening approached, Dr. Paetz came in with other doctors to examine me. He explained to Darla and me my situation and that I must recover at home for a month. Then I would need to have stateside doctors attempt another angiogram stent opening of the iliac artery. Should this fail it would be necessary to have a bypass surgery of the closed artery in order to save my left leg.

I asked if he was intending to release me to go home. He said if I could get through the night with no problems then tomorrow I could be released to fly home. No issues with flying so soon after this procedure, he said. As he turned to leave I called to him and asked if I could have a higher dosage of pain meds, as I am suffering dreadfully. He responded that would be okay now.

I asked how much and he said I could have whatever I need. He then left and soon a nurse came in with a small vial of a synthetic morphine derivative. She said this would last three hours or so. She gave it to me in the IV. Within minutes all my pain disappeared for the first time in days, if not months. Darla looked at my face after a time and said the entire locked grimace I had in my face disappeared.

I finally felt released and fell into a peaceful sleep. Blessed, peaceful sleep. As this night continued, the nurse would bring in a vial every three hours and I would have the most pain-free night I would enjoy for a long time to come. Of course we didn't know this at the time.

In the morning Dr. Paetz returned and examined the femoral artery incisions and proclaimed I was fit to fly. Then nurses came in to carefully cut away the sticky medical tape that was binding my groin up in a knot; it reminded me of duct tape. Finally I could stretch out. I thanked the nurses and Dr. Paetz for the morphine. I felt almost human again.

Darla had actually spent a peaceful night enjoying this part of Bremen and for once having some real stress-free time during this time of incredible emotional panic. I was wheeled out to the taxi and we were taken back to Stenum Hospital before my final check out.

Once the doctors completed their final exams, we got all our things. During this time I was still in a mild state of euphoria from the awesome morphine I'd had all night. This condition lasted all day as we concluded my stay at Stenum Hospital and the staff worked to get my flight changed, an absolute necessity to enable me to fly home with Darla. It was late in the afternoon that we left Stenum with many of the staff and doctors coming by to see me go, many in tears and with looks of deep concern clouding their faces but happy that I looked so well. They knew the struggle I will have ahead. But it was time to go home and face the future from there.

Darla and I arrived at the Hilton Hotel in Bremen, a short drive from the hospital. I had been given Oxycontin pills to take for the flight and I still had some pills left over from my earlier surgeries. I was now taking these to offset the pain that was coming back.

I had no feeling in my left leg; it was numb from the hip down to the foot. In fact my foot seemed to be incased in a sponge a foot deep. It was so odd to feel as if my leg was foreign to my body. But the pain was another story. The leg was on fire with every step I took so it was best to just stay in bed.

My left abdomen was another source of agonizing pain. I didn't know at the time, nor did anyone, that the surgery had damaged my femoral nerves. The later speculation was that the main nerve bundle had been severed. This caused me to have such great pain to the touch of my left side. It was intense misery. But additionally, the damage to this nervous system was affecting my heart rate and causing me to keel over if I sat or stood too long, and for me thirty minutes was too long. My blood pressure was measured three times when I passed out in front of doctors and it was so low, 40 or 50 over 20 or 30. Not good.

In addition to suffering from the two post-surgical problems of abdominal and left leg pain, was the emotional stress of finding out and the physical suffering caused by the surgeons placing this new larger set so far into the spine that it was impacting my L3 spinal cord area in the spinal canal. I had major pain blasting throughout my back, which was the cause of all my misery while laying on it in all these hospitals and for all the procedures. We only found this out later. So I was now waiting for our flight home.

Mr. Petersen at Stenum Hospital had somehow connected Darla and I on the same flight with Lufthansa leaving Friday, November 5th. We checked into the hotel on the night of the 4th and spent the night there reeling from all the events of my shattered body and broken spirit. Darla finally lay down while I drew a warm bath with some salts she had found and administered Heparin shots to my leg to prepare myself for the flight home. Heparin is a blood clot thinner that helps ensure clots aren't created from the long hours of sitting.

As I lay down in the bath my thoughts flew over and over these last fourteen days of the most insane hell I could have ever imagined. Here I was ready to go home with my wife, a truth I could barely believe. I was so emotional during this time. I was racked with sobbing over the suffering I had gone through, then praying to God for an answer.

I lay there giving my soul, my heart up to God and, reliving my life, I asked Jesus to come into my life to restore me. Whatever I had left in life I would serve Him. I asked this prayer and asked forgiveness of God for any of my trespasses. I asked God to let me make it home and if His will was for me to perish to let it happen there near my family. All this I asked in Jesus' name.

Only a short prayer yet filled with all my passion of having been stripped to the very marrow of a life, left with nearly all my energy gone. I was at the point of complete release, yet there was still something pushing me to go on. Was it Darla, my children, my mother, or my own desire to yet live some more? I could have taken all the pills and all the shots and ended it right there, away from nurses and doctors. I could do this while Darla was asleep, not knowing that I had taken an overdose of powerful meds for the last time.

But the will to live was stronger, and I thought my path not yet finished. I was at the lowest point of existence, in so much pain and agony just waiting for yet another wave of that insidious pain to erupt and lash my mind with its white hot burning endless whip of flaming fire.

I must have fallen asleep because the next thing I knew, Darla asked if I was okay; she needed to use the bathroom. I said I'm okay. I got up with her assistance and she helped me get to bed. I lay there waiting for morning to come.

November 5th, 2004

Morning. We call for a taxi and make our way slowly downstairs with my shaky body trembling at each step. I have loaded way up on Oxycontin so I can do this. The driver helps me into the car. We arrive at the small airport, and I am driven in a wheelchair to the plane, and soon we are leaving Germany.

What a feeling that was to lift off the ground and see the area around Bremen quickly grow smaller. I felt such relief and new anticipation. We flew into Munich and the airport officials were waiting for us with an electric car. We were whisked quickly through the massive Munich airport to our terminal.

The plane was waiting for me; yes, they actually held the passengers from loading; only the Germans could pull this timing off. I was taken from the cart to a waiting wheelchair and up onto a new Airbus jet. I was taken to our seats; Darla had stepped away to a small gift shop while I was being seated. So I was alone. Quickly the purser came up and asked if I was feeling okay. I am sure I must have looked like death warmed over. He must have been concerned I was passing away right there on his plane.

I replied, "I am fine, could you turn the air conditioning on?" He said, "No, you are not fine. What is going on with you?" I then told him about the surgery that had been performed on me, and that I had letters of release from my doctors. He then said he must get the captain to look me over. I was then dejected thinking that they would take me off the plane and put me back in a hospital.

Up comes the captain with a small black bag. He introduces himself as a doctor. I asked, "Are you a medical doctor?"

He replied, "Yes."

I said, "The airlines must pay more than hospitals." He laughed, examined me, and took my blood pressure. He then called the purser and quickly made arrangements for me to be moved into first class where the seats fold into a bed and instructed that I should be placed on oxygen for a time to see if my blood pressure would come up.

All this occurred while no one else was on the plane yet. The captain gave instructions for someone to find my wife and bring her up to the front of the plane. Let me tell you they had a hard time finding her, because I looked over seventy years old and they thought she must be that age too. So it was a humorous time they had locating her. Finally they found her and brought Darla to where I was lying down and was on oxygen.

In due course the captain came, near the time of takeoff, reexamined me, and pronounced I was fit to fly. He kept me on oxygen most of the flight and every couple of hours he, or a flight attendant, would check on me. What a relief it was to have this most caring concern happening right when I needed it the most, as I left Germany to return home to a very scary, uncertain future.

HOME AND
MORPHINE

———•—•———

Hours later we touched down in Los Angeles. What a mixture of emotions I had gone through on this flight. It was like waking up from a dream and wondering what was real. I couldn't know there were even more nightmarish events just waiting around the corner.

We were processed through LAX with me in a wheelchair being pushed by Darla, no electric carts with sweet young airport attendants here; just a cascade of people all trying to get out of the too-busy airport. But knowing I was in California was like drinking in the nectar of life after having been so far gone in mindless pain throughout these last ten days.

We made it to the car and Darla adjusted the seats so I could lie down to endure the long drive home. I was already letting go from the adrenaline from this event and the Oxycontin was not near strong enough to stop the new waves of pain that were forming in my body. We arrived home and what a momentous moment that was! I will not forget how wonderful it was to just

stand on my familiar property and see it again, a single mind picture. I resembled a dead man returning to life to view his past.

My children were so happy to see me, and my mother was
there to greet me. I was taken into the house and somehow
Darla got me upstairs to bed. I was getting very weak and the
pain was ratcheting up. Soon the excitement of coming home
relaxed as I felt such peace to be in my own bed again. While
going through those insane pain-filled days and the nights, oh,
those nights of horror, I thought I'd never be home again.

Darla and I discussed making an appointment with Dr.
Schnitzer as soon as possible. He was going to refer me to a vascular surgeon. She suggested we set this up the next morning.
Well, that never happened. As the night began, my pain became
a crescendo of additional force, a new animal of incredibly
insane torment. I tried to ask what pills I still had: Oxycontin,
Vicodin, Valium? But they were all like shooting at an enraged
grizzly bear with only a BB gun.

Within hours I was in such pain that my body began to convulse and shake; my wife and mother attempted to soothe me
with cold compresses and fluids, but to no avail. My convulsing
became violent as uncontrollable pain attacked my brain, crash-
ing through with unstoppable force that the feeble drugs I had
taken could not control. I was now thrashing back and forth in
the bed and sweat poured out of me. Darla dialed 911; all this
was happening in a brief period of time. In maybe two hours
I went from a resting state to a frightening person writhing in
bed in a fight against inhuman suffering. At eighty-three my
mother should never have been subjected to witnessing such
a terror. The paramedics arrived, took my blood pressure, and
called the hospital for instructions. My blood pressure was 225
over 110, a very dangerous level. The doctor ordered an injection
of morphine, which they gave me.

It took six paramedics holding me to control my thrashing.

They waited a few minutes and took my blood pressure again. It was still 200 over 100, another call, another injection. They were instructed to take me to the hospital. Six men lifted me from my bed and carried me down the same stairs I had emotionally climbed up just hours ago. I was placed on the gurney, strapped in, and given yet another injection. My blood pressure was still in the danger zone of causing a stroke.

The ambulance driver gunned the van through my neighborhood with my wife sitting next to me. We left my family wondering if they would ever see me alive again. In the ambulance the paramedics kept talking to the hospital and told the doctor the morphine was not working, my blood pressure was still too high. Another injection; we got to the hospital, I was wheeled in and given a large dose of DiLaudid, a drug many times more powerful than morphine. I was finally coming down from this pain stroke, as they later called it.

Once again I was admitted to a local hospital. This had become a very familiar routine for us and for them as they all seemed to know me. We all wondered how this could be happening. Darla was a wreck. I cannot imagine what she was going through. It had been only hours since our transatlantic flight. We were not even unpacked. We were dealing with home matters and jet lag. She had to stand there and watch me go through another crisis, with all the same unpredictability, a short time after arriving home.

Finally I was sedated. They gave me the best care, a pain pump with morphine, and at last I could rest. The doctors came in droves to examine me and hear about my overseas surgeries and the implants. They studied the films, took additional tests of my artery closure and were amazed. The doctor assigned to me recommended that I seek a referral to a vascular surgeon and discussed pain management. They decided it was best to keep me several days to monitor me, as this was such an unusual case.

This was a major relief for Darla and my mother. My family could not endure seeing this kind of scare again, and we had no idea as to the level of care I would require. Three days in the hospital would give us time to stabilize and plan the next move.

From the hospital my insurance carrier directed me to a local vascular surgeon. Unfortunately he was not attached to this hospital so I had to be discharged and taken to him. Darla was informed that they would set up an immediate appointment, and since I was doing better she could take me right away. I was leery because there were no provisions made for pain management.

The day arrived, and I was discharged to go. We collected my things and I was wheeled to the car and we drove to Santa Ana for the appointment. At this new doctor's office I was taken in and laid waiting on a bed. Finally the vascular surgeon came in and examined me. He stated that we had to wait until the intensive neurological damage and pain to my left leg subsided before he could do a bypass surgery. I asked about another catheter stent angiogram, and he stated it wasn't necessary and wouldn't work. Surgery was required, but it was necessary to wait, or the bypass wouldn't be successful.

We left bewildered as this doctor made funny comments about my German surgeries, and it was not comforting. As Darla got me in the car I began to tremble as the morphine was wearing off. Within minutes I began to shake and convulse as the pain waves began to hit. Again, the left leg, the left side and my lumbar back area were shrieking in agony to the now beaten and weary pain receptors in my brain.

I told Darla to take me back to the hospital as I was going back into shock. I was readmitted to the same room. Unbelievable. Back on morphine, the doctors were stunned. But I had told them I needed pain management to handle this. I must see Dr. Abraham. So Darla told the doctors she couldn't deal with me, and it was necessary that I be placed in a rehab facility to recover before the next operation.

A new twist and one that was uncomfortable, unnerving, and unbelievable, but I understood the trauma I was causing her and the family. I was calming back down and since I was hooked up to a morphine drip I was again content and stable. The nurses were happy I was okay and back where they could care for me. They knew my wife needed a break, and until I was given better home pain control I ought to stay there.

November 14, 2004

After a few days of pain management, the doctors decided again to have me seen by Dr. Abraham for home pain management. My brother-in-law Dan came and took me. I was covered in Demerol pain patches for the drive to Long Beach.

Once Dr. Abraham saw me, he was in his own state of shock over my condition, the latest news of the failed surgery, and the current dilemma. He prescribed the highest dosage of morphine sulfate he could, 240 mg a day, with 700 mg pain patches of Lidocaine to place on my left leg to locally control the pain. He also prescribed pills for depression, sleeping; you name it, I was now on it. A large box of medications was brought for me to take home. Dr. Abraham gave me careful instructions. It would be essential to exercise great care. This was the highest dosage he had ever prescribed. He hoped it would control the pain. Me too.

We started administering these medications immediately, and he instructed me to come back to see him every month for prescription renewals. He embraced me and I was a tough guy; he almost cried, I think. Dan and I went home. As I walked with a cane across my porch carrying a bundle of flowers, someone took my picture. This was a man who looked sixty-five instead of forty-five. The path ahead was grim. This fate was my new uninvited companion.

Mid-November

I have spent another two weeks in the hospital in addition to the two weeks in Germany. I am twenty-five pounds lighter and weak from the beating my body has taken. I cannot walk 100 feet. I am using a cane to move around and a wheelchair for any distance. I come home to begin this new home care routine. (Darla still wished for a rehab placement.)

The process now begins to recover sufficiently for the next surgery. Here I am, starkly different from a year ago when I was a guy on top of my world, in peak physical condition with strength, stamina, and flexibility that was amazing for a middle-aged male. When I look in the mirror I see an old man, invalid with no hope for anything but another surgery and who knows what will come next.

I am adjusting to my home care routine of massive drugs. I am so weak; I am only able to sit for short periods. I must lie in bed or on the couch. I try to do things, but even pushing myself to walk is a stupid move, as whenever I go past my limit of 100 feet, it brings on shockwaves of leg pain that no dosage of morphine will handle. Dr. Abraham had strongly advised me to not double the morphine dose like I had the Vicodin. He said that would be lethal.

So that was why I did something else; I doubled up on the pain patches until he found out and yelled at me. My next trick was to keep the old patches that might still have had some life left after the twelve hours of use and would put them back into the package and seal them up to keep them moist. Then I would reuse them with a new patch to get 2100 mg of this form of pain relief. Did this work? Who knows, but thinking it helped kept me happier.

December 2004

I am just waiting and waiting and thinking about my future. I am getting mad and sorrowful, too. I see the world going on around me and with the holidays coming it is a difficult time. Miserable though I am, I have decided it is time to act. My own will is about to resurface to take control of my own destiny.

Self Will

A month had passed since my last hospital stay, and I was getting into a routine of the home care drugs and feeling my body begin to recover, I started to feel that maybe I was okay, I could stop the whole thing, my body was fine, and that I could and should get off the drugs as the pain was decreasing.

Mid-December 2004

I reached an individual decision to get off the drugs. I sought no medical help. One day while everyone was gone, I decided to stop every one. Cold turkey. I had done it before and survived. Around the fifteenth of December I just stopped the morphine, the patches, and everything else. Then I waited. Hey, no pain! This was good. The day wore on and I didn't take my scheduled 60 mg Morphine sulfate contin, a time-released formula that is more powerful than just getting straight morphine. I was doodling, moving, thinking I was all right.

Later it began, first a shake and a roll. I felt queasy and weird. I started to have strange visions. Then I got really hot, I mean *hot*, so even though it was December I turned on the air conditioner and took off my clothes. I was burning up! In the next thirty minutes my body became freezing, really cold, chilled. Now I turned on the heat and covered up in blankets. Shakes, chills, and weird pictures going on at the same time.

Then I was hot again, back to no clothes and the air conditioner on. My daughter Bonnie came home and quickly realized something strange was going on. She checked on me, and I told her that I was all right. But thirty minutes later I was back to freezing and covered up in blankets with the heat blasting. This went on all day, over and over. Bonnie thought I was nuts. Now what?

This continued all day, every day, for three days. My wife was beside herself; she knew what I was doing. Again I was being a willful hardheaded guy. However, I knew what I was doing. The morphine became easy to stop taking. Going through these ten days of wild crazy hallucinations, hot/cold flashes, and shakes, I just hit the Vicodin and hard. Taking five, ten, then fifteen, then twenty a day. But I was off the morphine and I felt like a conqueror. I had beaten this, and I could now resume my life.

Next I weaned gradually off the Vicodin until I was down to only a tiny 60 mg morphine pill once a day to help me with my tremors which to me felt like being morphine-free, similar to an alcoholic who says but I'm only drinking only one shot a day, not five.

December 25, 2004

Christmas came, and I announced that I was drug free. Well, only since the day before, but no Vicodin and no morphine. I was done. I strutted and marched around like a warrior who had won a battle.

Our Christmas day events included driving to Santa Barbara for a family gathering. I was going to show them all my newfound recovery. I announced I was going to drive us to my niece's home! This was welcomed, even though I had not driven in months. I drove and it felt just like old times. I was talking, sitting, and all was fine. My leg hurt, but I ignored it. We made it there with no problems; I was somewhat shaky but the adrenaline was pouring through and kept me up on my own endorphins.

We visited, ate, and opened presents. After that I told Darla I felt strange and asked her to give me the morphine pill she had brought in case I needed one. I took the little 60 mg one. Soon I was feeling all right again, but told her I wasn't up to driving. She already knew that before I said it. We said our goodbyes and went home.

During the next few days I rebounded and cruised through New Year's. I realized I was holding my own. The use of my leg was still limited but I could now go 500 to 800 feet. This was huge. My leg was having continuous spasms and hurt, but I knew I was heading in the right direction. I was now controlling things with daily Vicodin, and I thought that was okay. I felt I could drive, so I did.

One day I went to my office to say hello. One of the salesmen thought it would be wonderful if I could look at a job with him. I said I would be willing. I drove to the job and, using my cane, made my way to the building. We joined the client and went for a walk, a long walk, thousands of feet of walking. Simple for everyone but me, this was my Achilles heel. I kept going until my leg erupted with new agony, and I had to stop. I said my goodbyes, went to my truck, and after a rest, slowly drove home.

Once I arrived home I placed patches on my now insanely painful leg and took a morphine pill. By the next day I was in full relapse, could not move, and was in agony everywhere; back, side, and leg. It was as if I had had a moment of glory. I stepped outside myself to be someone else, but then like Cinderella the midnight hour tolled.

The pain I was in was now beyond my worst, the very worst. Emotions from all this hit, and I was now in a terrible state. It was as if a vortex of evil had waited until I was most vulnerable and then sucked me back. I was back in daily agony, paying for a willful attempt at normalcy.

January 2005

I turned the corner from the success of defeating my monster only to have that monster arise and reassert its mastery over me. Morphine, more morphine; pain, more pain. Depression and crying over this incredible truth; I am finished and I know it. I went to see Dr. Edwards for this relapse and depression in addition to finding out if what the vascular surgeon had said was true. Dr. Edwards suggested I get a second opinion before doing anything.

Taking his advice I set up an appointment with a new vascular surgeon. As I now await this new appointment I begin to write again in my journal. I had started this journal the day I was injured back on December 1, 2003, keeping a day-by-day, and sometimes hour-by-hour, diary of my surgeries. Extending it to include many email messages to friends and family over the many months until my Germany surgeries. The impact of the failed surgeries led me to stop my journaling as it was too depressing to continue.

As I came to this new juncture of thoughts and emotions, I decided to record not just the events that occurred but also my innermost thoughts and heartfelt emotions. This was a poignant attempt to reveal the purest writing of my mental and spiritual state of mind. On January 30th I wrote the following journal entry after a break of five months:

Willie's Journal **January 30th, 2005**
Since my injury and through the long suffering of my many surgeries, I have been reborn again with Jesus Christ. I have

lived a full life with travels around the world and being happily married (we have had problems, as all couples) to my only wife Darla, who has borne our three children.

Bonnie is the oldest, a smart jewel of a young female, bright with the studies of education and idealistic with beauty to share her God-given talents with less fortunate people.

John is my only son, a boy all the way through, sharp mind, quick thinking for his age with great physical gifts, speed with quickness of hand to eye. Such a mind for math and numbers, he is our gift from God.

Hannah is a rose of love and charity. She is filled with a countenance of giving and sharing, which is rare. Her heart is as large as her energy to give. She's sweet and kind to all. Her passion is singing, along with a love of acting.

Darla is my wife, my friend and companion for 23 years. We have loved each other deeply, and we have injured each other deeply. Our differences seem insurmountable, but our love conquers all. Through these last fourteen months of extreme trials and suffering, Darla has endured and been strengthened. She has such faith in me. I love her with all my heart.

Today I begin to write this new journal, however poor my writing skills, and put pen to paper in my desire to record these emotions, thoughts, and revelations of my life and days that are of great value to me and to God. This journal (which is one of many) will be my spiritual journal.

My life has been greatly affected during these past months due to the injury to my spine on December 1st, 2003. On that date I suffered a terrible trauma to my back during my last session on a lumbar-strengthening machine.

During my lifetime my mother has always been a devout Christian. She raised my sisters, my brother, and me. We attended the local First Baptist Church and went to services even on Wednesdays. I remember around six or seven years old, being inspired to be baptized. This announcement astounded my mother.

I had my mother's influence in knowing the Bible stories and about being a Christian. In fact at age ten I attended a church summer camp in Vista, California. There, at a campfire with the youth pastor, I asked Jesus to come into my life. My father was not as outwardly devout a Christian as Mother. Indeed by the time I was 13 or so, he stopped attending church, so I did too.

Let's go back now to the military period of my life. Being in the Air Force, a man's world and with the separation from my parents, I gradually began drinking and, though not a drunk, these times were not Christ-filled. During boot camp you get physically toughened, no drinking at all. Once I arrived at the technical training base in Wichita Falls, Texas, drinking and other stupid stuff were more the norm. But I did not let it interfere with my studies, and I finished second in my class.

In October 1977, I was shipped to Northern Japan to Misawa Air Force Base in the northern section of Honshu, the main island. I also began my HVAC career here (Heating, Ventilation, and Air Conditioning). It was an exciting place to be, both for my new field and as my new home for the next 18 months in a foreign land. During the first twelve months I spent time listening to music, enjoying the local town's culture and food, and working out intensely.

Spent today reading deeply the Bible and a book by Billy Graham, *Answers to Life's Problems*. I meditated and prayed (something I haven't done much for a while) and thought of 1 Thessalonians 4:17 which discusses the resurrection when our Lord returns. Then I opened my Bible and while looking for 1 Thessalonians, I came across Ephesians 3:1–21. This is a powerful letter of prayer from Paul describing the promise of God in Christ through the gospel of the opening of God's grace to us Gentiles. In Chapters 1–3 Paul expresses God's plan. Chapter 3, Paul demonstrates to me the incredible love Jesus has for man and me.

We must open our eyes and heart to the truth. The only way to everlasting life is through Jesus. He paid for my salvation and yours with his perfect life and giving His life on the cross for all mankind! Thank you, Jesus! Even though I took Jesus into my heart again in 1989 with Pastor Harrington at Liberty Towers, my walk with God was still confused mainly by my selfish pride and belief in a masterful set of lies from Satan and his deceit-filled manipulations of the world and me.

Now my eyes are wide open and my heart belongs to Jesus Christ. My life is to serve God as He calls me to serve Him. I am deeply moved by the events in my life and the incredible suffering I have been through. If I do not survive this next surgery, I want to at least record this final rebirth with Jesus Christ as my personal savior. My life from here on is His.

So this was my journal entry of January 30th, which in a reflective time was to start the record of my own life events to give to my family as a parting gift. This was my sole thought and desire. Even before I had become apprised of the extreme risks of bypass surgery from the vascular surgeon, I knew I wouldn't survive this next surgery. I am now lying in bed sixteen to twenty hours a day as the pain is so fearsome in spite of the massive intake of morphine and the many other medications.

As the month of January closed I was preparing my family and myself through this simple method of communication with the intention that with my demise I could at least leave some record of my experiences, thoughts, and feelings to my family.

February 2005

Darla and I went to an appointment with a Dr. M, a certified vascular surgeon within my insurance network. We visited him and he reviewed my history. He is young and quite bold in his approach to my case. He agreed with Dr. Paetz that a second angiography should be made and was alarmed by the previous surgeon's reluctance to attempt this. He asks for his name and once I tell him he expresses astonishment as he informs us that this is a general surgeon who cannot perform vascular procedures like angiography. What incredibly alarming news!

With this information we decided for the second angiography procedure, and it was set for February eighteenth. I awaited this with much anticipation, as I was getting weaker and weaker and having great pain in my lower left abdomen. I could not sit or stand for periods of time greater than thirty minutes as I would pass out from low blood pressure. I was in constant pain, still staying in bed, hourly loading up on morphine.

February 18, 2005

The day arrives, and Darla and I are in the hospital getting me prepped for this second attempt. I had asked Dr. M if I could please be put under this time, because the first angiography in Germany was the purest form of hell and torture. He had assured me that this could be done.

Once in the angiography room I was lying on the table with the technician and nurses preparing for the doctor's entrance. All was hustle and bustle. At least here I could understand the language and know what was going on. They began to prep me for the incision, and I informed them it would take a load of local anesthesia. They scoffed at this. Dr. M came in right as they began to cut the first femoral and as I screamed, he jolted up and said, "You can feel this?" Of course, I replied, and we went through the whys and what for. They then repeated this two more times and he finally, just like in Germany four months before, said that I had to endure the pain of the incision as he could not give me more than the three shots.

I asked him when I would be put under. He said he could not do that. Another miscommunication and so I began to sweat the procedure knowing it would take hours. I braced myself with my weakening self-will and shortly, and I do mean shortly, Dr. M approached and said he was finished. I began to question him about what took place, but I passed out.

I awakened some hours later with Darla at my side in the recovery room asked her what happened. She said Dr. M tried three attempts and all failed. He wished to see us in two days at his office to go over the next option. I faintly agreed and after coming around in a haze from the medicated stupor we left to go home. Me in a blur of thoughts of what's next, and Darla in a wonderment of how this could continue.

More Bad News

<hr/>

February 20, 2005

Two days later we were in Dr. M's office, waiting for his entrance to explain the options. He came in after a long wait and, looking groomed for a photo shoot rather than a medical office visit, he went into a long dissertation on the previous vascular surgeon's diagnosis, his review, and a scathing commentary on the implantation surgery.

I asked about the planned surgery and Dr. M, without exhibiting any degree of hint of risk to me, told me rapidly how he would do a retroperitoneal approach, would put in a graft and I would be fine in a matter of days. With almost no consequence, he was that assured. I thanked him, and Darla and I left. It was right then that for the first time from the beginning of my ordeal that I stopped, and I began to ask God what to do next. This was the first profound moment of that quiet voice telling me to wait, and I listened.

So now it was back home and even though I told Dr. M I

wished to think it through, his office immediately began calling day after day to schedule the surgery saying that he had gotten approval from my insurance company. I was actually scheduled for this for a week later at the end of February. After much thought and prayer I told his secretary I was not ready, as I wished to get another opinion.

Finally after additional thought and prayer, I made contact with Mark Mintzer to inquire about his medical resources. He gave me the number and email address to Dr. Quinones-Baldrich at UCLA Medical Center. I contacted him, and to my surprise was given an immediate response and an immediate appointment for early March, just days away. I contacted my insurance company for approval for this third opinion and was given the green light from my new case manager.

As I was now in bed daily, letting go more and more each day, I was really getting depressed, far beyond what I had been. This was an ongoing nightmare of wondering when my leg would die, and if I would have a leg at all once the surgery was completed. I had now received Internet information on my type of injury, and it was very grim. Not too many people had ever experienced this, and those who had similar injuries to arteries had amputations. So I was getting no encouragement for the future of my left leg.

March 3, 2005

Today I have an appointment with Dr. Quinones-Baldrich at UCLA; a very significant day in my life. Darla wouldn't go. My brother-in-law Dan Petta takes me; he has been retired a year now and has been a great help to me. So we go. Dan pushed me in a wheelchair throughout the vast UCLA Medical Center facility located in Westwood. After a nominal time in the waiting room, we went to the examination room, and in a short time a physician's assistant came in to perform the work-up exam.

After this Dr. Quinones-Baldrich came in. He quickly strode up to my place on the bed and said, "Mr. Beeson, I feel like I have known you a long time, your case has preceded you with my colleagues around the world and on the Internet."

I replied, "I didn't know I was so famous." He then asked to check my foot and left leg as he was so intrigued by my case and thanked me for coming to see him. I was not too amused by this, but I knew right away he was a top surgeon and this was a most unusual case.

After the exam by Dr. Quinones-Baldrich, he described the plan for a sixth surgery, an aorto-iliac bypass. He informed me of the fact that there was a limited chance, due to this risky surgery, of survival. In addition I inquired as to the risks of loss of organs or limb, and he replied that I could lose my left kidney due to the mass of scar tissue and my left lung could be damaged from this surgery.

The real bad news was that due to my weakened iliac artery, the aspect of attaching an artificial graft to the artery, and a potential for non-adhesion, there would be a 50/50 chance of Dr. Quinones-Baldrich having to remove my left leg at the hip *during this surgery or even afterwards for up to a year!* So we now had the truth that Dr. M had not revealed to me.

Dr. Quinones-Baldrich then informed me that he was a specialist who routinely re-operates on failed surgeries and must redo them to improve the previous surgeon's errors. He informed me this was a highly risky surgery. I totally understood him on this score. Given the fact he appeared to be quite truthful and explicit in presenting the facts, even if he had to tell me the worst case scenario, I felt that he had, with his well-earned graying hairs, the seasoned experience that I very much needed.

The point of his being the Professor of Vascular Surgery for UCLA didn't harm him either.

We discussed how to do this and he informed me that my HMO insurance was not accepted at UCLA. I inquired as to what was; he replied PPO. I informed him I could switch to a PPO by May 1st. He then said we would have to wait and indeed, since my leg had not presented a necrotic extent, it appeared we could wait. I informed him I would contact him with my insurance progress and asked if we could plan for a May surgery date. He agreed to this and we set a date for mid-May for a pre-surgery consultation once my insurance was changed.

Dan and I came home with me having to digest this very involved and incredible new news of my options, now knowing the chance that limb loss was very real, and other organ damage or loss, and of course a high rate of not even surviving this highly perilous surgery.

LETTING GO

At home and I now deeply resolve that it is time to go through my affairs completely. As I arranged for my insurance broker to make the changeover for me at our company health plan roll-over date of May 1st, I made the selection of a PPO plan to match the UCLA insurance requirements. Amazingly our plan included a perfect match of a PPO provider that would allow me to roll from my HMO to this PPO. Another incredible step on this incredible journey and story.

Of course Dr. M's office was still calling me weekly to set up the bypass surgery that was approved with my HMO. They were very persistent. Finally I informed them of my decision once the PPO was assured to me.

Now the paperwork was done, and it was time to wait. I took care of all my affairs, trust, will, business succession, and then wrote letters to everyone beyond my journal. A slow goodbye, as daily I came to the expectation of my demise during this next surgery. Why did I wish to go through another, you ask? I guess I thought either it would be successful and I would get my artery flowing with a bypass and all would be successful or I would die. I didn't even think of a long recovery process with more problems. Just either/or.

My mindset, my decision made, and all my affairs put into order, I now just began the countdown to the day of my next appointment. However, these days were filled with numerous doctor appointments. I was taken from doctor to doctor because I was continuing to experience great pain in the lower left abdomen and was passing out frequently. So after seeing Dr. Edwards, who set me up with more specialists, I was scheduled for an upper and lower GI to find out what was going on with my innards, so to speak.

This was done in mid-March, so even though I was getting lower and lower in spirits, I was kept busy with more outpatient procedures, ultrasounds and MRI's to keep the process going. Undergoing tests, tests, and more tests. What were the new results? I had gallstones, nine of them, and the left femoral nerve to my left side had been either cut or severed.

As I continued through this slow spiral of more bad news, I came again to the conclusion that I was not going to get through all that was now proposed. Surgery number six to restore my left leg blood flow, surgery number seven to remove the misplaced ADR implants and fuse the L3-L4 vertebrae, and now surgery number eight to remove gall stones.

I mean, what more could a person need to hear to say *enough*? Now it was back to the hospital for a Hida-scan to find the exact nature of the gallstones and the condition of the gallbladder. This was done and confirmed per the GI reports and CAT's done a week before.

I was beyond asking, "Why, God?" I accepted my fate as the will of God. I did not curse Him or swear at Him. I felt that I was on this path for a reason and that there was somehow a purpose to this. However, I now prayed for the end to come in the next surgery. Even though I was putting on a good front to all around me, internally I was shutting my flame down one notch at a time with each new development of additional problems.

While I completed this swing of more doctors and procedures, I was still pumping myself full of morphine and barely able to function. I was getting so weak from lying in bed day after day after day. No strength and no reserve. I enjoyed having people around and talking to those who called me or wrote me. But the majority of the time I was down and out. Taking the medications. Counting the days to the next event. The bypass surgery was scheduled for May 7th, 2005.

Finally it seemed like everything was all in place. I just had to wait. I checked my leg many times every day to see if my toes were alive and well. I tried not to walk far. If I did walk, it was maybe 100 feet. I was basically an invalid in bed and someone brought everything to me: food, water, books, pills, and snacks. My wife or children brought up whatever I needed.

They were keeping a good eye on my needs and my state of mind. I was the one who was keeping an eye on my own lack of desire to live and it was becoming apparent to friends and certain family members I spoke with on a weekly basis. I was no longer the same driven, strong-willed man who so many people had come to know. I was now dependent, weak, drugged, and in great despair for my future. I was thinking only of the fact that my wife deserved a real husband, my children a real father, and that I was just in the way.

A Prayer

Mid-March 2005

During this particular time, my brother Harry called me and heard the news of more surgery and on and on. Harry listened and asked if I would do something for him. He then expressed his hope that I would accept an invitation to be prayed for by a spirit-filled and anointed husband and wife pastor team he knew.

He thought he could get them to come to my home. I balked at this and thought he was pushing it, for this type of Christianity was maybe for him but not for me. He then asked if I would consider going to their new church in Diamond Bar very near my home. Now I was very frustrated with Harry for this and told him no. Healings didn't work. He asked me to consider this. I responded that I would think about it.

I then hung up and was mad and upset. Why did Harry think this praying and hands-on stuff worked? I have seen it and heard of many people getting their hopes up, only to be still in pain or dead after the excitement wore off. I resolved to tell him no way was I going.

The next day came, and as I waited for hour upon hour of daytime to pass with checking my leg, my meds, my side, my colon in pain, laxatives, water, more meds on and on. Thinking about the major surgery ahead, I came to the realization that Harry may be right. I mean, I thought he might have a point. I am going to die. Not if, but when, soon, not long from now. I had gotten everything together: will, trust, insurance documents, all the papers of my life, diary, and letters to everyone hidden in easy-to-find spots once I was gone.

So I thought, *He is right, I have a chance for prayers for my family.* Not for me, since healings don't work in today's modern science-filled times. I knew it was just a money thing on TV. I thought praying for a friend or family member in need was good, and I certainly had many people do this during my ordeal, but this was different. It would be a time for me to have a sort of last rites before my last night. So I gave this thought and after a few days I called Harry and told him okay, never giving him or anyone the real reason why.

Now it was nearing the end of March. Harry and my family decided that Palm Sunday would be the best day. Harry came to our house to help Darla load me in the car and followed me to the church. It was called Father's House, a brand new church that had just that month begun to meet in the Diamond Bar Community Center. I was wheeled into the building and taken to the rooms where I could hear musical instruments being played.

Alongside me was my entire family: my wife, my children, my mother, my sister and Harry's family. Everyone who lived close, except my other sister Judy and some cousins. As they wheeled me into this room it was some minutes before the start of the services. I had told Harry I had fifteen minutes, then I must lie down or go home. He had briefed Pastor John

Park and his wife Pastor Michele Park on this condition. As I was brought in, they came up, asked my name, and introduced themselves to me.

I said hello and stated my name to them. There were maybe thirty people there besides my family. They asked me to be brought up to the front of the room and without much ado they, John and Michele, began to pray for me. It was happening so quickly. I thought they would ask me questions about my history, but nope, they just went right into this prayer and holding my arms.

John said almost immediately, "Willie, this was not your fault." This was like a thunderbolt to me. From the time when of this injury, deep down inside, I had wondered if I had somehow done something of my own error during the use of the machine and that I had brought the horror onto my family, not just the pain and suffering, but the emotional turmoil of all we had been through, surgery after surgery, and the intense loss of our good family times.

Additionally there was the harm to Darla and the toll she had paid during the many months of this ordeal. The impact was felt to our marriage, to our relationship, which was nearly gone as husband and wife, and as a father to my children. My ability to provide was gone. We were nearing total financial devastation with the loss of my income for one and a half years. Now disability income had ended, and no Social Security income, as that had not yet been approved, we were near the end.

All this I felt deeply and so it was a jolt, to have a total stranger tell me in a prayer that it was not my fault. I heard John begin to ask God to help me with my injury, to open the vessels to repair the damaged spine, the nerves, the tissues, the organs, and to allow me to rise up. But as I heard Michele and him utter these words for spiritual intercession, I began my own prayer. I shut them out and prayed to God. First I told God that I was finally in church with my family here children and mother.

As the pastors were intensely praying for my healing, I said, "God, why am I still here? I am no use to anyone. Not to my wife, my kids, my company, or to you. Just take me home to heaven now." I asked this of God. No, I prayed with force for God to come to me right then and take me home as I was in His house and I had given myself up totally to His will earlier this year. I was here and done, no need for another surgery. I said to God, "Let me go. I am finished, and there is nothing to gain from this." I asked God to let me die right there in that wheelchair with all my loved ones around me. My life was now over.

I heard John and Michele praying, and then a bright light hit my brain with force, a radiant beam of light coursing through my mind. I adjusted to this as a voice, deep, powerful, and clear said, "You are not going to die."

That was it. As it ended, I looked up to see who had turned the lights on and who had said this. I found that the sky outside was overcast and the blinds closed. The lights were on in the room. I then looked to hear that voice again from the people praying for me. None of them had that voice. John finished the prayer and I asked to leave since I was getting weak. I was taken to the car and I laid down as everyone wished to stay for the service.

I slept. After a long time I awoke and, thinking it strange to be there in the car, I got out of the car, got into my wheelchair and went into the building to find Darla to go home. I came inside and everyone was there. John came up and asked if he could pray again for me; I said okay. I was still shaken from the voice, but it wouldn't hurt for one more prayer, as I would be gone from here and would not see these people again.

So John and Michele prayed again, a sweet prayer for my healing. It was different this time as they prayed for our fortunes to change and for spiritual power. I thanked them, and someone took my picture with my family. I asked Darla to take me home, she did. I finally made it upstairs and collapsed on the bed in my own room, in my own home after enduring this prayer business. A sweet couple, but deluded, in my book, to think that they could help.

But I was troubled by the light thing, and that voice: who was it? I tried to see who said it and didn't hear that voice from anyone. Everyone was Korean there, and certainly it wasn't my brother. I was perplexed as it came right as I prayed my prayer to die. As I thought this through and reached for my pills to take, I saw a Bible sitting on the far side of the bed. It was Darla's. I reached for it and it opened up to Psalms and my eyes were drawn to Psalm 143 verses 8 to 12. Here are those verses:

Psalm 143

8. Let the morning bring me word of your unfailing love,
        for I have put my trust in you.
    Show me the way I should go
        For to you I lift up my soul.
9. Rescue me from my enemies, O Lord
        for I hide myself in you.
10. Teach me to do your will,
        for you are my God;
    may your good spirit
        lead me on level ground.
11. For your name's sake, O Lord, preserve my life;
        in your righteousness, bring me out of trouble.
12. In your unfailing love, silence my enemies;
        destroy all my foes, for I am your servant.

NIV

I read them slowly. I closed the book and set it down. I rested from the strenuous activities of this day. I was alone. Darla had gone back to the church to get the kids. After an hour, I rolled over and there was her Bible. I picked it up and it opened to

Psalm 143 again. I was startled and looked for a bookmarker; there was none. I read the Psalm and closed the Bible.

I laid it down and after a few minutes, thinking it was a coincidence, I picked it up and just flipped it open, it went right to Psalm 143. This was now getting strange. Every time I opened this Bible it went right to the same page. Every time. So I began to read that Psalm that kept leaping off the page over and over. Five times, ten times, twenty, thirty times and more every day. The Bible always went right to that page, unfailingly, time after time.

A TRUE ESCAPE FROM DEATH

———•◆•———

One week later the family was invited to my brother Harry's home for Easter. I believe he thought in his heart this might be one of the last times I might be able to do this. He lives over one hour away from us, and the drive going there was very difficult for me. By the time we arrived I was shaking and in great pain due to the bumpy ride in the car. I had the seat laid back fully, however it was still too much for me.

Once we arrived I was wheeled in, and I sat for a few minutes. I was in bad shape and asked to lie down. Harry put me in the downstairs bedroom, and I slept for over six hours. I finally awoke, and they brought me out. I sat with relatives for a short time. Harry brought me the book I had lent him, *Perfectly Legal*, the IRS tax book I had purchased the year before. I had completely forgotten about it. Anyway, we left soon thereafter and once home and back in bed I placed the book on my nightstand next to my bed for easy access.

The days passed by that week of late March with me lying in

bed, taking my meds, and reading this Psalm. It was so surreal this happening, like the voice and the light. I mean, what did it all mean? I sure wasn't going to tell anyone. At my urging Darla was packing for a trip to Arkansas to visit a family friend to get some much-needed R&R. She was near the breaking point from all this stuff. It was also a trip to find out if we could find a property there for a price where we could sell here and use our equity to buy there and pay off our debts.

It was our only chance to find a locale where we had friends, the price was right, and Darla and the kids could be happy. Me, I was not happy at all, just morose and moody over my life and the worthless state it had come to. As Darla flew out on that Thursday I began to get ill. I thought I ate something that didn't agree with me as I began to vomit.

This was no ordinary vomit, but a black, vile-smelling stuff that ripped my gut up. Of course I didn't think too much of it as it was just another passage of my ordeal. Every day at the same time late in the evening, my guts would tear apart and out would come this blackish mess, and the whole house would stink from this foul odor.

Darla came home on Sunday night and was immediately hit with this smell. The kids had gotten used to it. Darla ran upstairs thinking, she told me later, that I had succumbed and no one had looked in on me. Much to her surprise I was still alive. But, beyond death warmed over, she said. She asked what was going on and I said, "Nothing. I just get sick each night." So we called the doctor and he instructed us to go to the hospital right away. We packed and early the next morning (I wanted Darla to sleep some) we went. After a marathon wait due to local emergency room closures that week, I was admitted to the hospital.

Once there the cadre of doctors coming in to view me found my colon had gone paralytic, a condition prior to necrotic. It was quite close to the final time, and I was told another day or so of this, and I would have been gone. But they got it going again and were seemingly happy. They came in to tell me to get the surgery as soon as possible.

Then a surprise: the next day the doctors come in dressed in bunny suits; no, not for Easter. I was quarantined from everyone. They now informed me that they had tested my colon and had found I had a serious bacterial infection. They advised me that I would be in the hospital several more days and on massive antibiotics.

This was not good. I had left my pills at home and they weren't giving me any morphine, per orders from this doctor. I had to get nasty and convince Darla to bring some of my own in and sneak them to me to keep me going. What a stupid thing to do, but very necessary to stay there. I was now very depressed. All I could think of was the fact that now I could have my bypass surgery at UCLA postponed indefinitely.

I had called my partner to advise him of the fact I was hospitalized. I called him with the latest news and asked him to take care of my wife and kids with the succession, as I was not sure of the outcome. It shook him up and he said, "Don't worry, your position with the business is secure. All will be well if something happens to you."

I was relieved, as I was nervous that I could go at anytime from a setback with this infection. Every doctor had told me that infections were the worst thing to get over, and now, at this late stage, I had a very dreadful one. Something called Clostridium Difficle, a very lethal, last stage of life infection. Per my doctors, later of course, at this time they didn't tell Darla or me anything.

Now I was staying here and on massive antibiotics. I mean major horse pills. After four days of this, the main doctor came in and said my tests were now normal and I could go home! Was I elated! I called Darla and, after much confusion, we were discharged from my now over eightieth day in hospitals covering two countries. A wonder I was still here.

THE FINAL GOODBYE

April 2005

It is now the first week into April, and I believe I have become a hospital-bound human. I have spent so much time these last fourteen months in various hospitals with now three more surgeries to endure ahead. I believed this is my destiny, to live my remaining days in some hospital. Dr. Quinones-Baldrich had advised me that I could spend two weeks in ICU and three months in a rehab facility to recover from this next surgery. How I could ever envision coming out of this alive was very blurred to me at that time.

Now I come home, thank goodness, as I needed to recover from a very difficult hospital stay. Per my journal the care was not good (except for the food) as my meds kept getting forgotten and they even tried placebos on me. A waste of time! I can tell a morphine chemical smell in my body. They would just not give me morphine, but since I had my own stash there, it didn't matter.

I was my own nurse and doctor now from all the countless hours of being in a hospital with doctors and nurses, learning the routine, and what the meds are for. I had read everything I could to get up to speed on the methods of treatments I would be experiencing.

Being at home was the best for rest. I could now readjust my own morphine pills and get back into routine. I was also on a major antibiotic called Flagyl, 1000 mg. A real horse-sized pill. I was still in all my standard pain and nothing that had happened changed any of that. Made it worse to some degree due to the confusion of my meds and care at times. But overall it was a good thing I was there and received the care I did. I know my condition was so unusual, and standard care could not be given to me due to all I have been through. It was good to be home. Now it was back to the way it had been. I began to get calls as I got readied for a last month's wait and then the next surgery in May at UCLA. Things were stirring in the new insurance carrier application and changeover information from my old carrier. For once a smooth turn over, this was all available through our one carrier. We didn't have to change carriers.

One week after I was home, rested from the hospital, and getting some improvement in strength from the infection, my partner called me to request a long overdue corporate shareholder meeting to be held at my house due to my condition. He said it was for general business and to vote for the new director positions.

So we made it for the fourteenth of April in the evening. Darla made up some sandwiches and drinks for the meeting. I stayed in bed until everyone came. My partner, his wife, and our investor (my partner's father-in-law) arrived. Once all was assembled I came down the stairs and we got the meeting under way. It was not the meeting my partner had called. That was a ruse.

The true meeting was to explain the decision by the partners that they agreed to enact the disabled shareholder clause of our buyout contract and that I was being terminated as an owner, employee and manager, etc. Indeed they even asked for us to pay them back monies for the debt of the company to his father-in-law. It was a stunning shock.

I broke down emotionally, as this was too much to take. My partner insisted I sign documents in spite of my drugged state. I started to ask him what had changed in a week. Then he began to respond, and I said, forget it, as it isn't necessary, as they had made the decisions already. I requested that they not do this if it was going to impact my new medical coverage to the PPO. I was so confused and hurt.

I finally asked for a letter to explain why and then told everyone to leave. My partner accompanied me upstairs, and I asked him to leave. It was over. I laid down, cried, and sobbed uncontrollably for hours, racked by this incredible event of unthinkable pure greed. That after all I had done to build this company, in spite of its problems, that they would so cruelly take this path.

Darla consoled me that evening and thought to herself that this was the end to a man bit by bit stripped down in pain and suffering to the last shred of pride of worth to be taken in this most heartless, yet business is heartless, fashion. Kudos for them, nightmare for us!

As in a popular grow-rich book I read once, it stated that man used to kill animals to eat. Now in modern day he simply kills his fellow man through money and eats his lunch figuratively. An amazing analogy; as I wept for my loss and for my last shred of holding on to the only thing I had left outside of my family, my wife and children stayed close and comforted me.

Literally I cried for hour upon hour, tissue box upon tissue box until there were no more tears or feelings left. This was the loss and death of a man before the final event. I was now stripped naked as the day I was born with nothing left. No use to anyone and not wanted by anyone except my family who loved me and wished for my pain to end.

This was my state of being with three weeks left before surgery number six was to occur. A truly emotionally, mentally, physically, and spiritually broken man. Near lifeless, and with little reason to go on, only the mechanics of a lifetime of solving problems was propelling me forward one painful step at a time. Onward to the next event with no solution to be hoped for or wished for. To get into the surgery was my only hope now.

As a new dawn arrived, with the splendor of God's creation, I awakened to an inner peace. A peace I had not felt in many months, weeks, or days. Why this happened now? I do not know as I was so knotted in inner turmoil the night before of worry, strain, loss, and anger from the termination.

The ongoing question was, *How could this happen with people I had given my trust to for over five years*? I was shattered, but at peace, having wrung out hour upon hour of sobbing until the body could not pour out anymore. Business is business, they say, and I had just found out the harshest lesson during my lowest point in my life. Life is not fair, they say, not here in this world.

As this new day dawned I began to inventory my remaining life. The only true faith and loyalty I had was my family. My poor wife Darla! I had sacrificed our relationship so many times over the years for the business. To what now was this gain for? We were weeks away from ruin. We were now cut off from our company. I was deeply troubled that now I was going to lose my medical insurance and not get the PPO.

Plus, with the obvious months of care, the move of my family to another state was too much to take. So I began to re-inventory my future and the shelf came up bare. So bare that most of each day I was not able to truly function very well. This loss was the breaking point for me. I was so low in spirit and state of mind that if I had the means I am sure I would have taken my own life. The bare shell of a once-vibrant man reduced to an invalid creature called pity.

Goodbye was my mantra now; oh, I still read that Psalm,

it wouldn't go away. But I was in a dichotomy of terms of this schism of events and the voice of God telling me I wasn't going to die when all I needed now was that final goodbye.

More events happened. First, I began to seek counsel on my termination and it seemed that with me on the medications and signing a termination letter while disabled was wrongful on their part. So this began the process of knowing our rights in this new legal matter.

Second, Dan Petta, my brother-in law, was involved in a serious fatal car accident on April eighteenth, where the other driver suffered a fatal heart attack and crossed the median and drove head-on into his little truck. Dan was seriously injured and required an airlift and emergency surgery on his right ankle to pin the crushed bones. He was lucky to be alive. The air bags saved his life as well as the seat belt.

After he was released from the hospital, about the 24th, Darla offered to my sister to let Dan come to our home to recover, as he needed care that we could provide. Our daughter was now home from school and was able to help with Dan and me. Darla was still holding down a job, maintaining the kids and the household. Dan was confined to bed twenty-four hours a day, as he was roughed up pretty badly from his injuries. We put him in our son John's room downstairs, and Dan stayed put right there during this time.

THE VISION

April 24, 2005

We are all adjusting to Dan being here and getting his care set up with nursing. I am staying in bed mostly due to the intensity of the pain, my constant suffering to my back, my lower left abdomen, and my left leg. I am emotionally spent, beyond spent. I would say hyper-spent if there were such a phase. It seems the meds are now reaching a crescendo of tolerance and are not working like before. But with the new events that have now taken place, I am simply waiting for the next few weeks to pass with the milestones of May 1st, the new PPO coverage, and then the UCLA pre-surgery consultation with Dr. Quinones-Baldrich on May 5th.

On the night of the twenty-fourth I came again to bed after letting Darla sleep in the bed. I laid my head down and went to sleep after taking my nightly meds. I was in bed, asleep. The room was dark and all was quiet. A shining light in our room awakened me. I opened my eyes and could see bright red letters that spelled the words *Perfect Leg*; I looked to see where this was coming from. I looked through our window and then to where Darla was sleeping and could not see anything unusual.

I then reached to my nightstand light and switched it on and this red light on the wall disappeared. I could find nothing unusual so I switched the nightstand light off and rolled over to go back to sleep.

I was quickly awakened by the red light beaming again on another wall. I opened my eyes and looked again and there on the wall up high were the bright red letters, spelling the words, *Perfect Leg*. Now I thought, *This is weird*. I am really messed up on morphine, and this is another strange hallucination. I noticed it was coming from my nightstand. I looked there and was amazed to see that it was coming from the book, *Perfectly Legal*, only it said, "Perfect Leg." I then reached over, switched on my nightstand light, and this went away.

I looked at this book and recalled that just a couple of weeks ago at Easter, Harry, my brother, had given this book back to me, and I had set it on the nightstand. Now I looked at this book and realized that the lettering on *Perfectly Legal* was in blue. I thought, *This is strange*. I looked around and did not see anything extraordinary and no lights from outside the room, as it was dark. Finally, I gave up, switched the light off again and waited by looking at the book and nothing, no light, no red neon shone forth, just a book. I went back to sleep.

The next morning I woke up and looked all around to see if these weird dreams or hallucinations were continuing. I was now thinking I was losing my mind. As I explained this to Darla, she looked at me quizzically and thought I must be over-medicated and, of course, I was. So now I was losing my marbles.

April 25, 2005

I began a new journal book dated April 25. I then began to list many thoughts and ideas. My mind, this day, was racing with hyperactivity. I was writing thought after thought in frenzy it seemed that day. I had many ideas about little inventions, things to do, lists for the upcoming move, and all the repairs to be made to the house by others, of course. Dozens of continuous ideas flowing from my mind in a flurry of mental activity! It was very weird. I thought I was having more drug-induced phenomena from the meds. It was a strange day.

I continued to write in my new journal about the upcoming move and the fact that I would probably be in rehab while Darla sold our home and made the move with the kids. With Bonnie going off to college up north, this was the right timing, it seemed. I was back in bed and spending this day again, like all the others these many months, lying there wishing, wondering, and taking my meds each scheduled time.

That night as Darla came up to bed, I arose and left to go to the other room to let her sleep. I wrote in my journal and read. That was my typical activity, no TV. It was too depressing to see healthy people doing all sorts of things each day. I read books, magazines, technical stuff, medical books, emails, etc.

I also actually sent an email that night to Dr. Quinones-Baldrich requesting that Mark Mintzer be allowed to observe my upcoming bypass surgery. I felt this would be an insightful experience for Mark as he was becoming quite an expert now as a liaison to world-renowned surgeons involved in the complex surgery of ADR. That this would be a one-of-a-kind opportunity for Mark to see a vascular repair and help improve the industry standards worldwide; that was my hope. Mark was a most thoughtful and involved advocate to the ADR world, as well as a compassionate man, who had been through his own back surgery and knew the score.

This night, the night of the twenty-fifth, I finished my time away and finally came back to bed. It was about three AM. Here is what happened next; straight from my journal:

My Journal
April 26, 2005   **3 to 4 am**

To bed, I was much energized of late. I wrote many ideas as I lay in bed, just falling asleep, a strong surge of wind hit my consciousness. I looked at a barely visible door. An entrance of heavenly or magical appearance, it was some distance away and I saw a city of brilliant radiance past this immense gate. The gate was two giant golden pillars arching from huge bases and curved toward one another without touching in the center. There were large doors of a bar-like shape hanging inside these pillars, partially open.

The road I was on was brilliant translucent gold. Large pavers of clear gold, the most pure beautiful gold my eyes had ever seen. The city sparkled in radiant colors of a vibrancy no earthly eye has beheld. Emeralds, rubies, diamonds, sparkling as I came closer; I could see more detail and these precious stones were everywhere. Along the immense road, it was at least a quarter of a mile in width; there were many people, like guardians, along the road on each side, wearing brilliant radiant white garments, a pure bright blazing color. Many had long golden trumpets, and others were standing. I would estimate thousands of these beings were alongside the road.

There was incredible singing, music like I had never heard; the trumpets were blowing, the people singing. It was the most peaceful, joyful, loving place I had ever experienced. I viewed as I came closer. I was not walking on my own, and I was drawing near, feeling my way drawn there. I viewed the most magnificent buildings of pure white brilliance that hurt my eyes to see. I felt awesome power coming from the city of purity, love, peace, joy, and happiness. I felt overpowered by all this, as this all happened in seconds, if that long a space of time.

As I was seeing all this and hearing, feeling, drawing closer each second to the massive gates, I was instantly consumed by a series of mind waves of events happening so quickly, oh so fast! I saw my entire life blazed before me in a brief breath of time!

Wait, a voice. *You, Willie Beeson*; then I see there is a man next to me speaking to me. "No, your destiny is now to begin. You are free. God has heard you and blessed you. Your time has come, Satan's work is done."

He now turned to me, looking at me very closely, a man, very radiant and appearing brilliant. I felt such love and peace. He said, "Willie Beeson, you will be 100% healed, you will be healthy, you will be strong, you will be vigorous and you will be young!"

So much to ask, but I drift again to awaken and write down all this incredible vision. Hear these words: my life is God's to work, to guide. My body has been abused, injured, my pain tremendous. My family stressed, Darla, ill, hurt. Today I feel blessed as I haven't felt in years. So much has transpired with my back, operations, drugs, doctors, people, and needs with humans in pain. My hope was to get well and go back to my business, and then they came and have taken it away. What now?

My prayer is for God to lead me, to guide me, fill my heart with love, my family to grow, be nurtured by love, and that we can live peacefully together. We, watching Bonnie leave, can see her begin a new path to learn the truth of her own path, grow in knowledge, and help others.

For Darla and I, to enjoy a time of healing and peace; I feel like a deep burden has been lifted. I have been so afraid, so fearful of losing, becoming broke, no money. Now I have gained through this time of renewal for my deeply injured body, to live through these days of medical reversals that had no hope, each passage a new burden.

Why me? Darla and I together again, we can be like two freed lovers grasping our life ahead with our loved and blessed John and Hannah.

So beautiful, so honest, together our lives intertwined with love, happiness living as God-like faithful to our Lord above. This time, all at once, is my final passage through death's door to freedom, hope, love, and life. Please, oh, Lord Jesus, we pray to our Father in heaven for mercy and forgiveness as we go forward with this next operation that your will be done. And for my little ones to have a father in me to guide, teach, praise, honor, cherish, nurture, and love each one. This is my one desire to be here, alive, vigorous, and healthy, in love with Darla, seeking your glory with your protecting angels around us to carry us forward to our future. With all my heart and soul, I bow in prayer to you, God, thank you for your mercy and love to redeem me, a sinner through Jesus' sacrifice for mankind. In my hell I have passed through, I loved you ever more and give my life here this day to you, Amen.

Vivid dream? Nightmare? Vision? Only God knows, and that is all I need to know. Thank you, God.

Time for a pause and a reality check as I wrote this down in my little journal book. I was so shaken by this and dazed. Even though it was near 4 AM, I woke Darla up to tell her about this incredible dream—no, vision, as it was so vivid. Not like a dream, as it was too brilliant and powerful. She awoke and thought I was having another attack or something. I told her the vision; she sleepily said to me (considering the "Perfect Leg" thing) that I must have doubled my morphine dose.

So I realized she was probably correct, and I turned to the nightstand where all my meds were and turning on the light opened the bottles of morphine and other meds and counted away as I continued to write this amazing vision down. Darla went back to sleep, as I was not in any danger. I counted those pills and realized I had taken the proper ones and quantity. I finished writing this down, and I fell asleep too.

In the morning Darla went to work. After she left I woke up, and being all alone upstairs, I needed to get up too. I arose and stood; I reached to my back where the pain was so severe from the implants pressing my spinal cord. And to my amazement there was no pain as I made this upright movement to standing, whereas all the times previous it was driving pain.

I then reached to my lower left abdomen and felt the acute area of hypersensitivity where the extremely damaged nerves were. I felt this area and pressed it hard, no pain. I now felt that my left leg was hot and it pumped. I reached down and felt that, instead of my leg being cool, it was warm. It pulsed to the touch. I then stood erect, and I mean erect, for the first time in months. I walked downstairs and in my pajamas went outside with no cane or wheelchair.

I walked straight to the sidewalk and standing there I knew. I knew I was now healed; the vision was *real*, and *God was real*! I then walked and ran my entire neighborhood, over a mile! Praising *God* then and now. As I write this book eighteen months later, I am still weeping with joy and gladness. This moment was the most serene, joyful, amazing moment in my life. I was freed, healed, and filled with the love of a Creator who had heard the prayers of so many and gave me back a restored body. This was a day like no other.

I wept, I laughed, I ran, I stood, I walked, and I could do anything again. I felt no pain anywhere. I was incredulous. Amazed and dazzled. Like a death row inmate who, awaiting the last call, looks up and the gates open and is told, "You are free to go." This was me. I was instantly healed, not progressively, not will be, but now, right now!

I was beyond myself in mental and emotional breakthrough.

I mean, who had ever, in this era, heard of such a thing, and it had happened to me. I cried and laughed and was probably looking like a very weird person running around in my pajamas. Leaping, lifting, doing anything I could think of. Just being outdoors was exhilarating, freedom to live again as a whole person.

I ran into the house to see Dan and tell him the news. He was not sure of the truth but could see I was moving like a wild man. He cautioned me to slow down. My daughter observed me and thought I was being very bizarre. Finally Darla came home to see me in the backyard breaking up bricks and using a very heavy sledgehammer. She flipped out. Bonnie flipped out. I was flipped out.

As the next several days came and went my strength was alarming. In fact within two or three days God sent all my muscles back. From a dependent, weak, flaccid tissue body, to ripped steel-like bands of muscle. God's honest truth, my son John would be sitting with me on the couch and my legs and arms and body would begin to vibrate at a high rate of speed, he touched my arm and leaped back and said, "Dad, I got shocked!" This was the very time God was reactivating my tissues. Each day this occurred several times. Even twisting my spine to new positions I was getting stronger and stronger and with flexibility that was not there days before.

Each day I would wake up from a short nap, and instead of pain I leaped from bed with moves that would challenge a gymnast. I was daily getting younger and fitter and stronger. Instead of lying in bed sixteen to eighteen hours a day, I was nonstop energized those same hours. Not sleeping, just taking a short break to sit and catch up for twenty or so minutes, and then going again for eight to ten hours.

How does one explain this to others? It was the most awesome, yet bizarre, event. Happening right in front of my own family, yet it was true. I could walk miles and miles. Yes, I had leg pain from these walks due to the incredible atrophy in the leg muscles. But I could go like the wind and walk distances unheard of for someone with the occlusion that was there days before. I didn't know anything about how or what had occurred. I knew what God had said through Jesus, and this was a miracle. I was healed and well and healthy, getting stronger each day, younger and fit with vigor that even in my best times could not be equaled.

God is real and so amazing in His love and care for us. I came to Him in my lowest hour and asked to die to let someone new take my place in my family. I prayed to somehow avoid the next surgery with a fearsome recovery ahead. My prayer was to take me home, God. Do with me however you must for my sins and my not honoring you. But let me go.

This was my heartfelt prayer. God responded with telling me I was not going to die. Then, knowing I was dying with the bacterial infection, which I was soon to find out in the days ahead, was a fatal infection almost 100% of the time. How could all this happen? The timing of my partners taking away my last hope for a return to my own place of worth (so I thought) to the "Perfect Leg" sign?

Then the most incredible event of my being taken to heaven to God's home to His holy city to see my life forward and backward, to hear those words, "You will be healed, strong, healthy, young, and vigorous." Then it all came true. How does one deny this?

How does one accept this? Certainly it doesn't take one long to realize you are whole again. But instantaneously? With no pain at all? Able to do anything I desired? Stopping all those drugs cold turkey, as I did not take anymore that day or since. With no withdrawals, this is a mystery. Like God is a mystery. But God shows His wonders to us every day. We choose to ignore the beauty and the wonder of a marvelous Creator who desires us only to thank Him and to honor Him.

Why me? I only know that I asked to die. God wasn't ready

for that, and I wasn't going to do it myself. Our will to live is God given. Men can take it away, but without a bullet to a major organ we can go on with disease, pain, suffering for years. Can anyone be healed? I think so, once you let your will go and let God come in and seek His kingdom in your heart.

How could this be, you ask? I know because I came to that point of complete nakedness of self and was forced through all these events to come to the point of no return. I sought God my Creator my Maker to end it. As He made me, He should finish me. He decided to remake me. I know in my heart that God, who is grace, love, and purity, responds to His children with blessings. We are full of impatient pride and want it now. God is sovereign, and He alone knows when we are truly humbled and obedient and deserve in truth His justice.

God is sovereign, not a pushover Deity, but a forever, true God. Did I deserve this? For me to say yes is pompous. I didn't understand why He would do this for me. I asked God why me, why not others who I thought deserved this far more than me. The response? It was for your family and for those people who prayed for you in remembrance of me.

God is no fool, but a wise infinite being who is real. This is no joke, no strange but true man made or invented thing. How does a man go from being incapacitated from multiple surgeries, on massive dosages of drugs the most powerful made, with crippling injuries confining him to bed or a wheelchair to instant health? Deny God doesn't exist.

For those who are believers, stand in awe of His mighty wonder. I do. I thank God daily. Hourly at times, as I cry to Him that I cannot ever give to Him what He has given to me. Try that.

Those incredible first few days zoomed by in a new life for me and my family, and the shock of this new event, a mysterious occurrence to those who couldn't get the awareness of my vision.

Yet to my children who, as children are the voice of truth, when asked by my wife, "What do you think of Dad now?"

They responded, "He is playing with us."

Adults take time, kids are so aware of the world and the instantaneous aspect of this existence and they don't doubt God, not when young. They don't have their minds filled with adult nonsense, as I call it. Later they will be like the rest of us, like I was, a pre-occupied believer in God. Not anymore, I am like a child now in my trust of my Maker and His will for me. I am here to serve Him with my life that He alone has given to me to live in a path to serve Him.

EUPHORIA

Now back to this impossible miracle and the events that followed this incredible healing. In the immediate days following this I was taken up with so many insights and thoughts and, I guess, mini-visions of heaven, life, people, and the accompanying euphoria that would naturally follow a mind-blowing change like this. We have all heard of or seen cancerous tumors disappearing or other diseases mysteriously clearing up.

But this instantly strong and healthy return to life and living was one of a kind. I was soon to find out from doctors, family, and friends, the total amazement and disbelief that I was fine. A man who had spent eighteen months enduring hell over and over with each event leading to more dismal and frightening news. How could a person recover so quickly? God, but for those not ready for this, it was mysterious.

Within days I was riding clouds of a glorious return to life. First, it was to experience all the privileges of life, like walking, smelling flowers, yard work, driving, oh, driving, that America lifestyle achievement. What a moment that was to drive again, drug-free and healthy. Taking my kids to school, going to the grocery store. Visiting my mother.

Oh, was that a day to go to her condo, knock on her door, go in to see her in bed, and wake her up with a look of startled amazement on her face that only a Polaroid could and did capture. That day pulled her out of depression for me and got her on track again. She was the first one.

Then my son's Little League teammates' parents and coaches. Those faces when I showed up with John for a practice day a few days after my healing. I was running, throwing the ball, and catching like a kid. A jaw-dropping day for those folks.

To calling my brother to say I was healed and his disbelief and then I drove to his office and walked in. He went crazy and for all the best reasons, a perfect validation to him of faith in prayer. He was elated and ecstatic to have a true demonstration of God's love right in his own family.

Saw Dr. Edwards in early May to inform him of my change and to see his reaction and his staff's. A moment they or I will never forget. He found a pulse in my foot and proclaimed, "This is incredible!" But the real moment was his telling me of the knowledge that I had walked out of the hospital a month before with an infection to my colon that few survive. Dr. Edwards kept repeating that, and the fact that he had called his staff together that day I was hospitalized. He said a prayer for my family as he said to me that he knew he would never see me again. I was moved by this true compassion. He was smiling as the nurses came in to express their honest amazement at my recovery and healing. I told them all how it happened. Dr. Edwards wrote it all down and advised me to go to the spine and vascular surgeons and show this to them. I said I intended to.

He could not believe I was no longer on the meds and that I had stopped cold turkey. He took my blood pressure and was surprised at the steady normal rate. The warmth of my left leg, with the blood flow, and the lack of pain in my body! He advised me to go slow and to get opinions from my specialists and then come see him again.

More people, more amazing responses, neighbors, friends, employees, a continuous line of people who had seen me in the way I was and now. Whoa. One of the best was my good friend Mike Meskell, a good friend and a strong Christian man. He had counseled me with his sage insights as to my decisions through this ordeal right from the day I was injured. Throughout the ongoing months he would visit or call and check on my care, my thoughts and my state of being. Mike would pray for me and keep me in prayer chains with his church and men group. I was impressed with his devotion and care for me and felt his love for me even if we were not lifelong friends. I felt that he was a true embodiment of Christ's teachings.

So it was another great day in early May to call Mike at his work and tell him I was healed; He was very busy and thanked me and praised God quickly. He said he had to go. Then the next day at seven AM, an unusually early time for Mike to call, he called and asked if he could come over right away, he was very emotional. I said sure.

Once at the house he saw me and was crying and shaking and happy and praising God. He explained that when I called he was so focused that it didn't sink in, until late that night. He awoke at midnight with the realization of what I had called him about and he then couldn't sleep until he could call me. He was so mad at himself, but once he saw me he was humbled, thankful, and he visited for a long time that day.

Mike witnessed a quick unplanned demonstration of my new strength as I had been filling large trashcans on wheels with broken bricks. My kids were helping and one was overfilled. No one could move it. Neither my kids nor Darla could. Mike tried and it was too heavy. He suggested we take a load of the bricks out to be able to move the can.

I walked over and Mike asked me to not try to move it with my bad back. As he said this I easily moved the immovable can and wheeled it away to where it would be out of the way. Everyone was speechless, and then it hit them that I was not the weak and incapacitated person from before. I was not gaunt or pale or flaccid. God had given me ripped muscles, and I was strong and vigorous. Again, I am not trying to boast, just to testify to this amazing event of God healing a sick man.

Indeed, this same week, I cleaned out our garage and attic, lifting extremely heavy boxes and crates from the attic that I had placed up here years before. I put these in front of Dan who was now recovering quite nicely and could now sit in our living room. He was speechless as I walked in with these large boxes and crates that weighed easily close to one hundred pounds.

I was in euphoria of God's grace. Nothing was now impossible for me to do. Another act of grace was not another act of strength, but one of love. As Mother's Day was approaching, I began to devise a day-by-day inspired plan to shower Darla on this day for all that she had endured. With this tremendous impact to her life, I wished to thank her like never before.

I began to purchase items one after another, expensive gifts, which we couldn't afford, but I was in euphoria and not thinking money anymore, just freedom, God, and thankfulness. As each day went by I made these many purchases. Of cosmetics, lingerie, lotions, perfumes, roses, dozens and dozens of roses, a watch, a purse, a wallet, a necklace, and a very large ring.

I planned this perfectly to secure all these items and on Sunday, Mother's Day, I made an excuse to come home from church early and set up all these gifts on the lawn with balloons galore. The wrapped boxes were all on a blanket with her favorite pictures surrounded by over one hundred and eighty roses. It was incredible. I wrote loving cards and placed each gift carefully on the blanket.

I set up the camera and waited for her to come home. She finally came, and was she stunned at this display. I guided her to the chair to sit down. Then I started the camera going and the kids now gleefully handed each gift to her and she opened each with tears and joy and fear over the money spent.

It was straight from my heart to her for her loving patience, tolerance, suffering, and endurance for this most incredible ordeal that we had lived through. She could have left me. So many other spouses I had heard of did leave when faced with this major a reversal of life, of fortune, and of suffering happened. So I was very much desirous to show her my love, even if we didn't have the money, I did it anyway.

Eventually Darla, in practicality, took most of the expensive items back, kept some, and traded others in for more useful things. But we do have the video of this remarkable day as I was healed and doing all I could to show her how much she meant to me.

I didn't have to tell this private matter in this testimony of my healing, but to me this embodies the complete turnaround in my life, of the meaning of what was the most important thing to me next to God, and that is my wife.

Would I do this again? Yes, only I would let her choose the things she wanted and let her agree to the cost, which is what we did this year on this Mother's Day and for her birthday. It was a new day and a new life beginning for both of us.

Back to the story as it continues to unfold with one amazing event after another. The various doctors who have been caring for me kept testing this miracle. Going to UCLA on May 12th was going to be the best and brightest moment. They had called to back it off one week, and I didn't spill the beans of my healing. I wanted to surprise Dr. Quinones-Baldrich.

May 10, 2005

However, I did ask Mark Mintzer to come over as he had just come back from Germany, and we hadn't spoken for weeks. He agreed and was eager to hear why I sounded so good over the phone. He came in and was visiting with my brother-in-law Dan downstairs, when I bounced down the stairs and came up behind him. He turned and I gave him a hug—well, it is better to hear it from him, as he wrote this email to the back pain message board that day. Here it is:

I had lunch with Willie today. Drove to his house … knocked on his door … let myself in and talked to his brother-in-law while I waited for Willie.

> I was expecting him to come downstairs with a walker or cane. The last several times I had seen him, he looked like death warmed over. He's been in such bad shape for a long time, I was expecting the worst. He appeared behind me … I turned around and gave him a hug … being very careful not to hurt him. He embraced me with a strength that I did not think was possible.
>
> After the initial shock wore off, I stood in disbelief as I looked upon a healthy looking man … not ashen … not gaunt … not frail … not forcing a smile through a grimace of pain. We walked out to his truck and I asked about his pain … "What pain?" he replied. I expressed my disbelief, and he stopped his truck near some very large trash bins that were on the street. He picked one up and flung it around … twisting and bending. I went and picked it up … it was heavy.
>
> He's been off pain meds for 2 weeks … dropping massive doses of morphine-sulfate, cold turkey, with no withdrawals. His back pain and leg pain is gone. His abdominal pain is gone. There is still some claudicating (leg pain with exercise) from the occluded artery, but it's

not serious enough to keep him from coming back to
life…enjoying every second. He attributes all of this to
the power of faith and prayer. I'll leave it to him to explain
the details. I don't know how to explain it…I'm just glad
to see my friend looking happy and healthy. As we ate
lunch, I couldn't keep my eyes from leaking…it was so
good to see him like this.

What a great day!

Mark S. Mintzer

Global Patient Network

P.S. Willie…take it easy!

[May 12, 2005, 07:19 PM]

Mark and I were, and still are, quite close as two men who have
had similar experiences in life with back surgeries. Mark had just
started his small advocacy business to help back pain sufferers when
I invited him to accompany me to Germany. We spent a long flight
and the first night together in the hotel discussing my upcoming
surgery, neither one of us imagining the road that lay ahead.

As my horror unraveled Mark was there, step by step with
the doctors and hospital staff, insisting that my care be given the
highest level of attention during this most extraordinary ordeal.
I will never know what Mark actually did, but I do know he
went through what few non-family members would or could
go through. He did this and stayed with it, even after he had
to leave to go back to the states. He interceded with the surgeons there and even collaborated with top vascular surgeons
for opinions so he could help my family and me to make the
proper decisions.

This was beyond the typical advocacy relationship and,
indeed, in Mark's many trips to Germany since then and the
many surgeries he has seen and assisted his clients through, he
still relates that mine was the most severe trauma he has wit-

nessed. It sends chills up both our metal and bone spines to think of those hours and days of crisis times that were emotionally, physically, and mentally traumatizing to him and me.

Mark has a unique perspective and a difficult job in his field. To help those who are nearly beyond help. He has to console and deal with the failed surgeries that can and do happen. So his real emotions are shown in that truthful message to a group of fellow back pain sufferers who had joined me in the camaraderie of the moment as I suffered this horror.

This day, May 10, will forever stand out with Mark as the day he personally saw this handiwork of God and the truth as so many others have seen and you are too, of a loving Father in Heaven who responded to a plea for help and gave a life back. I thank Him for His grace, and I honor Him with this story.

LIFE ANEW

May 12, 2005

Now we go ahead with my incredible new existence and the UCLA appointment. Instead of Dan taking me, I drove myself to Westwood, walked unassisted to the building and then, after checking in, was taken to the examining room. The best ever was Dr. Quinones-Baldrich coming in and stopping as he saw me, sitting on the bed looking like the Cheshire cat with a big grin.

He exclaimed, "What has happened to you, Mr. Beeson?" I started to reply, and Dr. Q says, "How do you feel?" I reply I feel fine. Next he asks, "How is the leg?" I say it is fine, too. He hesitates then says, "If you are fine, and the leg is fine, then we can and will postpone surgery." I could have kissed him. He then asked me to tell him what happened. I did, and he then said it is a miracle, and that they have seen miracles before at UCLA.

He then orders a new ABI test of the blood flow to the left leg, and once this is done, he comes in with the result and is amazed. He says it has come up almost thirty points. This has never happened without surgical intervention. He asked me how the pain is. I reply it is not too much. He asks how far I can walk and I tell him miles. (See the report in the appendix for the actual UCLA documentation of this amazing day of days.)

I have included there the actual examination by Dr. Quinones-Baldrich and the ankle brachial index test from that day. As the report shows my right leg was a resting index of 1.3 while the left was a resting index of .82. This was up from a previous index seen in the other ABI test in November 2004 of .54.

Again, this is a subjective test and results can vary. But the facts do not deceive here. The blood flow was substantially improved and this was clearly not due to any other intervention than from a loving and caring God who had intervened to perform another awesome miracle, to add to the infinite number of miracles already performed.

Need I tell you here that the reaction of Dr. Quinones-Baldrich was one of sheer delight and utter incredulous response? He actually took that report and called in several other doctors to show them this miracle, and proclaim to them that I was scheduled for an aorta to femoral bypass surgery with problematic results. Now I was walking miles each day with little discomfort, whereas the last time he had seen me I could not walk 100 feet without agonizing ischemic pain.

It was a moment for a Polaroid, which I had and took another memorable picture of Dr. Quinones-Baldrich beaming with the reward of seeing a human being who has been given the gift, through the grace of God, of an awesome miracle.

Below is another post from Mark on my way back from this appointment:

> I'm still wiping away the tears...I just spoke to Willie again. He is on the way back from the vascular surgeon's

office. He had changed insurance and waited for months for the switch to take place so he could have the best of the best operate … Dr. Quinones-Baldrich at UCLA.

The relevant number is the ankle-brachial index. It compares the blood pressure in the ankle to the blood pressure in your arm. It had been 0.5, or low enough to worry about losing his leg. The test today showed it at 0.82! Something has caused the occlusion to open up. I am so happy for Willie … a few weeks ago, it seemed that he had no chance for a life … just an endless stream of medical challenges. The surgery they were planning is serious … the colon problems were serious … everything was serious and there was no end in sight.

Now, he's feeling fine and has every reason to look forward to living again. Willie has been incredible through all of this, demonstrating grace and courage that I know I don't have. Willie, YOU ROCK! I'm so proud to know you and am so very happy about your success. I look forward to a long friendship and getting together without any talk of medicine!

Love,
Mark

www.GlobalPatientNetwork.com

May 18, 2005

It was now on to Dr. John Regan, my spine specialist, who although he had not performed any of my surgeries was equally as important to me as if he had. He was, since my return from Germany, providing my ADR care and advice as to my next potential surgery. I now traveled to Beverly Hills for this appointment.

I was taken to the room, and a PA examined me with amazed

reactions and had more X-rays taken. Then Dr. Regan came in and exclaimed that he had heard of my healing and asked if I was here to show off. I said, no, I am here to get his opinion on my spine and its condition. He examined me and questioned me as to the vascular surgeon's consult. I explained to him the result. Dr. Regan said this was incredible and if true that a major artery had opened, then it would be a medical first.

He asked about my ischemic pain, and I told him what I had told Dr. Quinones-Baldrich, that I am walking miles each day, even being just three weeks since the healing. Dr. Regan asked then about my pain and the amount of meds I was on. I said no pain. He looked at me quizzically and said, "What about the meds? How much are you on?"

I said, "None."

He said, "That is not possible."

"I haven't taken any since April 25."

"I cannot believe this."

"Would you like for me to bring in the full bottles?"

He then looked at me and said, "No, I believe you, but if what you are saying is true, then this is a miracle. Certainly the amount of morphine you were taking was massive and with all the other meds, stopping cold turkey would have caused an immediate cardiac arrest in anyone, even Lance Armstrong."

I said, "Well, it is true, no meds, no withdrawals."

He spoke with amazement in his voice, "This has to be divine intervention." He then proceeded to look at my new X-rays and told me I was fine. He asked to see me in three months. I asked if I could be released to work; he paused and said, "No, I want to watch this for a time, at least one year."

I was aghast, and said so, but he refused to budge. He said this was because it may be a healing event, but now my recovery is to start and there is great emotional and physical recovery still to be made.

So I left this appointment realizing that my doctors were taking a very conservative position in spite of my obvious new condition; both doctors had commented that I looked great, younger, healthy, and vital. Not the aged, gaunt, weakened man that they had seen just weeks before.

Now I began a time of renewal, of living life and being a whole person again, only with a totally different outlook on each day. I gave God thanks for this miracle every day and began to live and enjoy and do those things that mattered. I also told everyone this incredible story. But new emotionally challenging times were just starting, as we were now, Darla and I, in a quandary as to direction. She was determined to move and sell our home here in Brea so we could start fresh in Arkansas. I thought we should hold off, as we had been given this gift. We were at loggerheads with the crisis of lack of money being the biggest stress. We were daily going back and forth on this struggle.

One day in early May, maybe about the mid part, we were seated at our son John's Little League game, me in a chair, she in the bleachers. As we relaxed the subject of no money came up and that we were now just 6 weeks away from zero money. Darla insisted we move, and she wanted to place the house on the market soon. This was our only hope. I was telling her that God didn't heal me to leave us stranded and broke. We needed to put our trust in God. Unfortunately this went over like a lead balloon.

She thought I was still mental from the Mother's Day extravaganza, and she was the only one thinking logically. I was getting an eyeful of daggers from her. I continued to tell her to trust God. Right then, as she began to tell me her position, my cell phone rang. It was a close friend of mine, a fine Christian man. He said to me, "Willie, I was just praying. God told me you and Darla needed money."

I said, "Yes."

He said that he would come over right away to give us a

check and would continue to give us a check each month for whatever we needed until I could go back to work! A loan with no interest, I was flabbergasted. I told him to hold and handed the phone to Darla and asked her to listen. He told Darla the same incredible news. She got off the phone, looked at me and grinned, "I think our life is different now." I agreed. Now we had no more money problems to worry about.

The next phase of our life was that once our children finished school in mid-June, we purchased a truck and a small travel trailer, loaded it up and went on a ten-state, two-and-a-half-month-long tour of the western states. We decided it was the best thing to do, considering that we truly needed to spend time together as a family and have positive experiences once again.

We took our little ones to Idaho to stay with the grandparents, Lita and Larry. Darla and I went on a solitary journey to see this great land and to discover more about our path ahead. We drove over nine thousand miles, and all that with zero back pain or leg pain or any pain. The only pain was from mosquito bites along the Yellowstone River in North Dakota.

Our trip throughout these states and just spending time together was essential even though it was difficult due to an uncertain future as to what I could do and when. Obviously the termination from the company weighed on us; certainly we wanted this to be done with. And we were now in the thick of the legal action with them and the doctors' office where I had been hurt.

For a while though, it was important to travel and put our issues on hold and get renewal. We went to Idaho, Montana, Wyoming, Colorado, North Dakota, South Dakota, New Mexico, Arizona, Nevada, and, of course, many parts of California. It was a trip of a lifetime, and it was the best thing to do with all we had on the plate and all that had just left the plate.

This was an important time for both of us to pray, to read, to sleep, and to see the beauty of this country, to have time with each other and time alone with God. Especially in some of the most spectacular parts the USA. We could have continued this trip for much longer than we did, but family responsibility called and we came home in mid-August to California to face the future.

GOD'S VALIDATION

August 2005

We are now back home from our wonderful freeing trip around this beautiful land we live in. I immediately packed up and took Bonnie to her first year at school in Northern California. I drove up, got her into the on-campus housing, spent a day walking the campus with her and going around shopping for her. Then I left and drove home, another thousand-mile turnaround. No pain.

September 2005

In mid-September, I see Dr. Quinones-Baldrich again. He is amazed at my youthful appearance and health. He asks if I am lifting weights; I laugh and say no. He examines me again and says the pulse is stronger in the ankle, weak in the knee, but nothing in the groin. He then says it is due to new collateral arteries having formed to provide blood flow. I ask for a CAT scan but he declines. He says I have been through too much. He then pronounces that the surgery is now elective not a required surgery. It will be my decision based on quality of life for me. If it gets worse or I cannot take the daily pain from normal living, then I can go ahead with the bypass surgery. But he said if it were him, he would enjoy what he could from life without the surgery. He also told me I must walk daily until it hurts to keep the collaterals open or they will shrink and cause me ischemic pain like before and stop me from walking again. He wants to see me in six months.

On to Dr. Regan on September 18th. Again he is happy for me. However, he has bad news. He has reexamined my films and announces that the L3-L4 new implant is poorly placed and is incongruent. It is riding on the rear part of the plastic core and not on the center. He feels this will fracture the core and require another surgery! I said when? He said who knows, a week, a month, a year or five or ten. We don't know. I asked what I could do to prevent it. He said no bending, no twisting or lifting to compress the spine as that would cause an overload and damage the core rim and could fracture it.

Then I would have to have a new revision surgery to remove the pieces and do a fusion. I was hit hard with this. In fact he had a counselor sit with my wife and me. Dr. Regan said again how he won't release me and will see me in April '06. He advised me to go slow, and he wanted me to start physical therapy to strengthen my truncal area and my abdominal muscles, which would help to relieve the pressure on the L3-L4 implant.

Another appointment; I saw Dr. Edwards to explain all of this. He concurred with the specialists. However, he was concerned mostly about my gallbladder and sent me back to Dr. Smith for a new evaluation.

October 10, 2005

I visited Dr. Smith. He was amazed at my complete healing. He did a most thorough exam of the anterior surgery sites and felt it was awful. I have massive scar tissue and they destroyed my abdominal sheath on the left side. He checked me for hernias and said I must be very careful to not lift or carry weights. He then checked the gallbladder and said if I am not in pain we can put this on hold. He ordered an ultrasound. He will call me with the results. He said go enjoy life, keep recovering, and continue physical therapy.

Late October the ultrasound is performed. Waited a couple of weeks for results, and then finally called Dr. Smith. He called me back and was confused by the report. It showed no gallstones and the gallbladder normal! I asked how often this happens; he said never! Another miracle. So I went to see Dr. Edwards and this blew them away too as they had never seen it happen either.

January 2006

I started new physical therapy exercises and suffered a flare up that was very painful from the lower back and left side through to the buttocks and leg. My leg had severe spasms during these new exercises, and we stopped after the second session. Dr. Vertson, the physical medicine doctor, said I should go to Dr. Edwards and get X-rays. I did so. Dr. Edwards ordered a full set to take to show Dr. Regan and a Doppler ultrasound. I am in tough pain for the first time since the healing. Hard to move at all! Dr. Regan put me on Mobic, an anti-inflammatory medication.

The technician doing the Doppler found I had normal artery blood flow in my left leg through the groin! This is not possible! Not with the iliac closed! So after this I was dazed and ecstatic.

The next day I go to see Dr. Regan with these results. My

back and leg have calmed down to a slight ache. Dr. Regan looks over the X-rays and looking somewhat mystified says to me, "Have you seen this here, at the L3-L4 level?" I said, "No." He then tells me that the vertebrae have auto-fused with a halo-like formation surrounding the implant. You can clearly see this on the films. I asked, what does this mean? He responds that he will not comment until more tests are performed and he immediately orders a lumbar CT scan. He then looks over the Dopplers and orders a CT angio-scan of my left leg and hip. He sent me to the facility for these tests immediately. I drove over to Beverly Hills for these new tests and then went home.

Two weeks later I went to see Dr. Regan with my friend Fred Korte, for the results. He looked at the new lumbar CT very closely and pronounces my L3-L4 auto fusion is amazing! It has formed in the anterior area not the dorsal position of the spine. He shows me that it has formed completely around the implant. I asked him about the surgery; he informed me I would need last year. He responded that it is stable and secure now and the core will not come out or fracture. I asked what I could do now with my spine. He said anything I wish, since it is perfectly healed.

Dr. Regan was very composed but he was quite moved about this event, so I asked him why he was so puzzled. He responded that when an auto-fusion occurs and it is rare, it happens in the dorsal area. This anterior growth was a first. He also replied that for a small amount of bone growth of an auto-fusion it would take two or three years. Mine had happened with a major amount of bone encapsulation in months, not years, since it has been only 13 months since my last surgery. I asked him about the films he took on May 18th last year, three weeks after my healing, and could we view them? He asked why. I responded, to check for the auto fusion. He retrieved them and once we viewed them, he exclaimed this is not possible! The film from last year showed the fusion had already clearly formed *only three weeks after my vision*!

So then he looked at the CT anigo-scan and said this was not possible. The iliac artery (left) comes off the aorta and then it disappears in the complete occlusion. In a few centimeters (5 to 7cm) the artery reopens with *full flow*! He exclaimed again that this was impossible!

I said, what did this? He said there was no explanation, and it was a mystery. Well, he said it is explainable by God. He then said I am an enigma to the medical world, as this was not possible. Fred yelled that I have a guardian angel. Dr. Regan said, yes. So I asked, can I be released? He said go see Dr. Quinones-Baldrich at UCLA with this and then six weeks after that to come back and see him. If he concludes the same then Dr. Regan will release me.

What a powerful event! I am so stoked and alive with a fully vascularized (working blood vessels) leg and a stable spine. Like new, it seems a perfect leg and spine. I feel so good. Praise God!

March 2006

I visited Dr. Quinones-Baldrich for the follow-up to the CT angio-scan as Dr. Regan ordered. Dr. Quinones-Baldrich came in and asked me what the symptoms were in my leg now. I asked, "In what way?"

He said, "How far could you walk before you have pain?"

I answered, "I have walked over 12 miles without pain."

He snorted, "That is incredible! Doesn't it cramp?"

I said, "Well, if I don't walk for a week then the first half mile is tough, but as I continue to walk for another mile or more it goes away. I have been running up hills and stairs."

He and his PA were impressed. He said, "Well, what do you need me for?"

I said, "Dr. Regan wanted this follow-up due to the unusual report on the angio-scan CT."

He looked the film over and commented that I must have collaterals somewhere, but they can't be seen. He looked and couldn't find any, but feels in his scientific cause that there must be some below my pelvis. There aren't any, I told him. He then said, "Well, it is done. I cannot do anything for you now." I thanked him for his help. He then stood up and said, "Let me check your leg."

He then examined me and found a pulse in my upper groin (no one has found a pulse there in 14 months) and he exclaimed, "This is it!"

He was very happy and his PA said, "His pulse in the foot is strong!"

They were pleased and Dr. Quinones-Baldrich said, "When you have something made perfect, why bother to try to improve it?" I understood he meant the ultimate physician, God! So I left elated and very happy and gave thanks to God for my incredible healing and my *perfect leg*!

April 2006

My next appointment was in April with Dr. Regan, my spine surgeon in Beverly Hills. He examined me and took more X-rays. All was fine. In fact he gave me a full unconditional release as to my spine and told me I am a complete mystery to him. He was happy for me, and I asked him if he would help me on my book; he said he would.

Finally I am arrived. I have now come full circle and it is so awesome. I can go to work soon. I set up my final appointment with Dr. Edwards, and in late April I went to see him and in great spirits handed him the release from Dr. Regan. Dr. Edwards took a step back and asked about the consult with Dr.

Quinones-Baldrich. I told him the results. He looked over the angio-scan CT and pronounced he cannot release me without more feedback from Dr. Quinones-Baldrich. Additionally he may order more vascular testing to understand how the artery is flowing past an occlusion. I am mystified, as I thought that Dr. Edwards would automatically release me.

But he has justified concerns, and he is right in his position that if I go to work for some company and my leg fails on the job, he would be liable. It is that simple. So no release and back to my rethinking the future. I have been interviewing with companies and each prospective employer is waiting for the full medical release.

May to June 2006

After much prayer and study, I come to the realization I am to go back into business for myself. God is really leading me to this. I sent in for my license to be reissued. At first I was declined my license by the Contractor Board, but then they came back last week and said they would reissue my original number; this is significant.

Then the license was issued in mid-June, months early; I scrambled to keep up with the immediate work that began with the heat wave of June and July. It has been so awesome as I have done physical work that I haven't done in years, and it is like I have the stamina of a twenty year old twice over. No pain, no stiffness, and no meds. Just exhilarating physical activity and I am in business once again and providing for my family.

I am fine and living a good life, and since April, I have shared my healing testimony at several churches and with many, many people I have met through my business. Clients, vendors, people at gas stations, as I have been working long days and nights in excess of sixteen-hour days, six days a week, all at a pace that would stop a much younger man.

POST-SCRIPT

Now you know the rest of the story, my story. I have written this lengthy and verbose journal of my incredible story of going through hell and coming back again. I give thanks to God, our wonderful awesome God. I pray for those who are in pain that God will heal them too.

Still to this day I do not know, why me? Is it due to my own supplication to God? Was it my wife? My children? Or the many thousands of people worldwide who had prayed for my pain to end? I only know that today I am a different person with a perspective that few achieve in this life. I give thanks for God for His being an unfailing source of freedom from worry and fear of the things of this world.

Is this because of my facing the most hideous pain and suffering that could come a person's way? If so, then why didn't this happen months earlier, rather than having to go through all I did? All I can say here now is that if you had seen what I have been privileged to have seen and felt and know throughout my conscious the truth of our God and His world, you would have my perspective that this world is small and fleeting. That we are here together not to hurt each other but to help and to provide willingly with care, with love, and with truth.

I am not a pastor, I am not a theologian; I am just a common person with an uncommon journey. With a most incredible belief and respect for our God, who despite all the wondering of man at why He is hidden from us physically, that He lives!

With my new life each day, I give thanks. This is the greatest change in my life from who I was to who I am. I thank God for all He did for this great life of abundance, of beauty, of wonders, of His greatest creations, and of His presence in my life. I see what I could not, and I hear what I did not, or tried to blot out. God is good and wants only for us, His greatest creation, to acknowledge Him and seek Him with our hearts.

If I could tell you one thing, it would be that He is real and seeks us. He needs us more than we could ever possibly know in our feeble ways. Our God is pure love, unconditional love, even for those of us who feel God hates us or that our lives are ruined with no one, not even God, to help. Yet, we are the ones who deny Him. We are the ones who throw Him out. Yet, He welcomes us with the purist love and forgiveness of a parent who has welcomed a lost and now found child.

Is it so simple? The answer, people, is, yes. Seek Him and the reward of knowing Him is joy. When you listen to Him, you will have peace. Peace that transcends all knowledge. It isn't found in machines or technology or achievements. It isn't in money. It isn't in the finest education. It certainly isn't found in food, yet that can be a close second.

The truest peace of our lives is acknowledging that there is one who is more than us. One who is here for us. One who will help us. Only we have to ask for this help and then follow through in honoring this amazing person who has helped us throughout our lives, even when we denied He existed.

Again, I am not a theologian. I am a simple man who has been given the grace to live here my way, and then go through a journey of suffering to see how wondrous our life is here with God rather than here without God. Living godlessly is a dangerous life filled with pitfalls that are real, not imagined, and that area is filled with anger, pain, hate, deception, and death.

How can it be that just acknowledging that there is one person, a supreme being made up of spirit, who actually came to earth in the form of us to give His life here for us so we could be with Him in His world, even after we rejected (and still do) Him.

Yet here we are, each of us in our own ways, each day running around with so little thanks to this being who made all of this for us with nothing asked in return. Not even taxes or gifts or a thank-you card. Just a whole magnificent world of billions of amazing species, creatures, landmasses, oceans, air, sun, moons, and stars, all made for us to have.

Yet we daily abuse this and take this and complain and criticize each other and condemn the other guy for our faults. Amazing that our God would give of Himself to save such harsh folks like we have evolved to. Yet, He loves us. I had to find that out in a painful path that led to God hearing me and bringing me to Him to hear that I was okay, that I was loved, that I would be fine, that my body would be healthy, strong, and my destiny would now begin.

What a charge to hear that! Our God, that far-away object of such intense discussion by billions of people, right next to me, in His house, in His world, my world too, my future world, your world, if you seek Him. Today, right now, it is easy to simply ask. For once in your busy life to look inward and say, "God, I have forgotten you. I need you. I ask you to forgive me as I do forgive those who in my path have hurt me. Let your son come into my life and restore my soul to the beauty that you created it to be. A soul that is full of charity, of hope, of radiance, of life, of grace, and love that I might be your servant and seek you in all I do. I know that Jesus came as a man and died for me, and still lives. He is your Son and is my Redeemer. Forgive me, Oh God, and fill me with the peace that transcends all."

Seems nutty, but that is the plea that works. I did it through my nightmare of pain and depression. I could not stop the journey I was on. Only God could. Only God can. Ask God to help you. Be patient, as it can, and does, take time. Remember God doesn't look at a clock like we do. Give to others first and see what occurs in your own world.

In closing, I would like to say to you, the reader of this true story: thank you for the time you took to look into my life. It may have seemed unreal; it was to my family and me. I seek no personal ego drive for this, only to show to each reader the story of a life that went through such pain and suffering and yet was incredibly miraculously restored only by God. This has been the impossible miracle for man, yet a gift of love from our Father above.

EPILOGUE

To complete for you, this amazing journey, the reader of my story, I have been asked by my publisher to compose this epilogue. This day is significant, October 23, 2007, as I reflect on my thoughts three years ago on October 23, 2004. I, with all hope and trust was preparing for my fifth surgery in the hospital in that most beautiful part of northern Germany.

Later on that day, I lost the total usefulness of my once strong body. The waves of pain are etched in my memory. The hopeless looks of those around me, the nurses, the doctors and my wife, hour after hour of endless mind numbing waves of pain. This was that day.

How can one look at this without wonder? How does anyone who has joined me in the telling of this story not be deeply affected by those events, all my hopes, like your hopes anxiously waiting for a solution, the solution to end this passage. With all the amazing technology, the recorded acts and works of mankind, there is nothing but faith to take us through an unknown moment ahead. Who knows what is ahead of us, in five minutes, one hour, a day: no one knows, only God knows.

As I lay in that bed in Germany coming out of this latest radical operation, my mind began to absorb the new information as events raced with doctors and tests to determine my new complications. What does one think of? I can tell you. One thinks of wanting this to end! At first it is the situation, the loss of being, then it is the pain, the endless continuous waves of pain. How could I have been so blind? Or was there no other hope for me? This is our only thought for hope, and hope for an end to it, for changes, for it all to go away.

Within these days of endless nights of torturous pain and fear, my body racked with one horror after another. Something occurred. The beginning of the reshaping of a man occurred; to lose his faith and his belief in man to asking for help from his Maker.

From that day just three years ago, as you have now come to know, my life was lived with great suffering. I, with you, marvel over these words that this journal has recorded. Today, I am pain free. I am strong, healthy with a vigor that is at times unstoppable. My world, my family, my vocation all restored. My wife has a real husband. My children, a real father, my family a son and a brother, completely alive and well.

As I take this all in, this Job-like story, my story I am compelled to look at this like it is a dream. How could this be? Yet it is! For those who believe this story, for those who have their own faith in God, you know as I know, our God is alive and real. For those who prior to reading these words did not believe, well, my hope is for you to acknowledge that this mystery can not be explained; it is not impossible! Believe!

Figure 1 William Beeson with daughter Bonnie @ Thanksgiving 2003, five days before disk rupture.

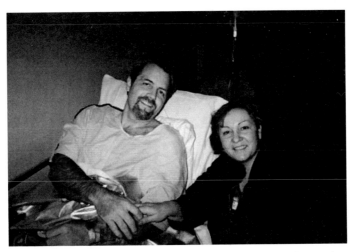

Figure 2 William Beeson with his wife Darla on December 23rd, 2003, getting ready for surgery #1 in hospital.

Figure 3 William Beeson January 2004, getting ready for surgery #2 in hospital.

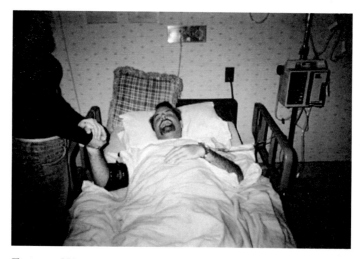

Figure 4 William Beeson January 6th, 2004. After surgery # 3, in hospital room heavily drugged.

Figure 5 Slide of Charite SB III artificial disc device. Photo courtesy of Dr.Willem Zeegers @ www.zeegersadr.com

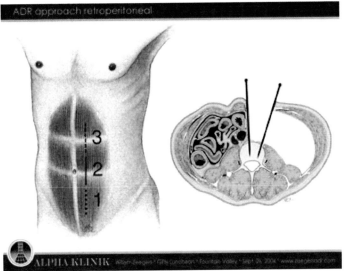

Figure 6 Slide of approach of surgery to implant ADR device. Photo courtesy of Dr.Willem Zeegers @ www.zeegersadr.com

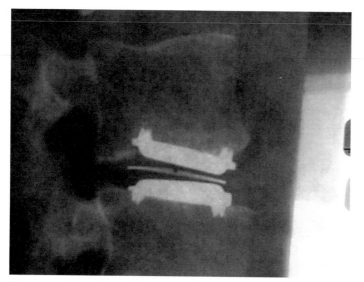

Figure 7 X-ray taken September 2004. Shows the L3-L4 implant is subsiding upward into the vertebrae.

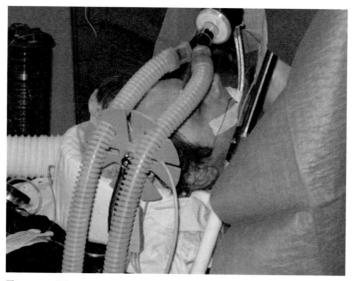

Figure 8 Photo taken by Mark Mintzer of William Beeson on October 23rd, 2004 going in to operating room in Stenum for revision surgery #5.

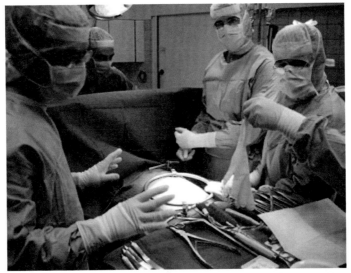

Figure 9 Photo of William Beeson on table in the operating room in hospital for revision surgery #5. Note Mark Mintzer second from right.

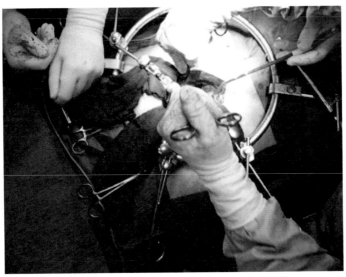

Figure 10 Photo of William Beeson's actual ADR approach during surgery #5.

Figure 11 Photo of implant taken out of William Beeson's spine during surgery #5.

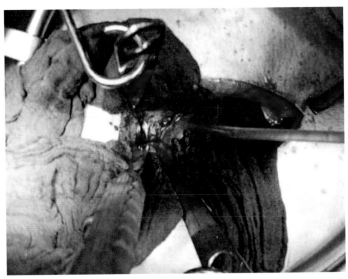

Figure 12 Photo of new implant placed in William Beeson's spine during surgery #5.

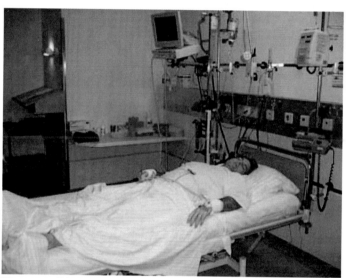

Figure 13 Photo of William Beeson in ICU after surgery #5, when no pulse in left leg is discovered.

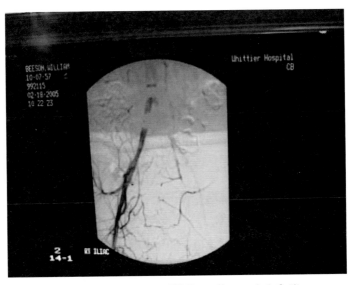

Figure 14 CT x-ray showing William Beeson's left iliac artery is occluded. Note this film was taken in February 2005, four months post surgery where occlusion occurred. Implant device obscures aorta and right artery in this film. Film clearly shows left iliac is stopped near bifurcation of aorta.

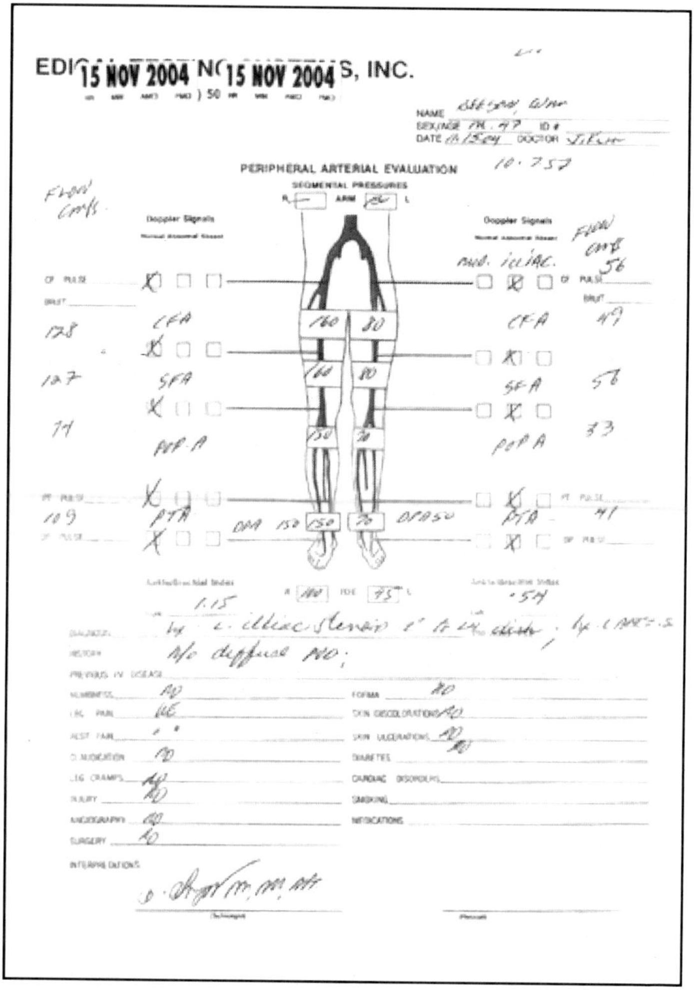
15 NOV 2004 15 NOV 2004 S, INC.

NAME
SEX/AGE ID #
DATE DOCTOR

PERIPHERAL ARTERIAL EVALUATION
SEGMENTAL PRESSURES
R ARM L

Doppler Signals
Doppler Signals

CF PULSE
BRUIT
CFA
SFA
POP A
PT PULSE
PTA
DP PULSE

DIAGNOSIS
HISTORY
PREVIOUS ... DISEASE
NUMBNESS
LEG PAIN
REST PAIN
CLAUDICATION
LEG CRAMPS
INJURY
ANGIOGRAPHY
SURGERY
INTERPRETATIONS

EDEMA
SKIN DISCOLORATIONS
SKIN ULCERATIONS
DIABETES
CARDIAC DISORDERS
SMOKING
MEDICATIONS

Figure 15 Ankle brachial test taken November 14, 2004 shows left leg has ABI of .54.

Figure 16 Photo of William Beeson on his porch, home from hospital November 14th, 2004.

Figure 17 Photo of William Beeson in wheelchair March 20th, 2005 at Father's House the day of the prayer.

Figure 18 close up of William Beeson in wheelchair.

Figure 19 Cover of Perfectly Legal book by David Cay Johnston. Note "Perfect Leg" reference.

VASCULAR SURGERY CHART NOTE

BEESON, WILLIAM
ID: 353-16-13

Date of visit: May 12, 2005

Mr. Beeson is a patient who is status post five back operations. The last one complicated by occlusion of his left common iliac artery. The patient has been extremely symptomatic in the left lower extremity with symptoms that were likely secondary to both vascular insufficiency and some degree of neuropathy. The patient has been advised to undergo an aortoiliac bypass however he had some insurance issues and now that these have been resolved the patient comes back for further follow up. Upon my arrival to the room the patient states that he feels fine, that there is no further symptoms in the left lower extremity and that all of them have resolved. I asked him how far can he walk and he states five to ten miles.

The patient informs me that he went to healing session a few weeks ago and after some prayer within a couple of days all the symptoms went away.

On examination, his blood pressure is 124/80, temperature is 36.2, and pulse is 96. His weight is 185lbs. His abdomen is soft and non-tender. There is no distention. Femoral pulse is normal on the right. There is a trace palpable femoral pulse on the left. I could not feel popliteal. There is a trace posterior tibial pulse palpable on the left. Dorsalis pedis is absent. Pulses are normal in the right lower extremity.

Both feet are cool with 3 to 4 second capillary refill.

Mr. Beeson clinically feels much improved. I have recommended that we obtain ankle/arm indices for further documentation. As I have informed him, regardless of the results of the ankle/arm index, given his remarkable clinical improvement I do not believe that intervention is indicated at this time. I have recommended to the patient that he continue to ambulate on a daily basis a report any changes. Otherwise, we will see him again in three months for follow up.

William J. Quinones-Baldrich, M.D., F.A.C.S.
Professor of Surgery
Division of Vascular Surgery

WQB:rw

Figure 20 Actual chart note from UCLA of May 12, 2005

Page 1 of 1

353-16-13   WW   UCLA Medical Center
BEESON, WILLIAM A   Noninvasive Vascular Laboratory

Peripheral Arterial Examination

Date of Study: Thursday, May 12, 2005
Type of Study: Ankle-Arm Index

Diagnosis: Claudication
Requesting Physician: W. Quinones
Technologist: Eugene Hernandez, RVT

Age: 47 Gender: M

Brachial Pressure: Right: 146mmHg Left: 146mmHg.
ANKLE PRESSURE: Right: 192mmHg Left: 120mmHg.

Resting Index: RIGHT: 1.3 LEFT: 0.82

Audible(0-4, 0=Absent, 4=Triphasic)
Posterior Tibial Artery RIGHT: 4 LEFT 2-3 Dorsalis Pedis Artery RIGHT: 3 LEFT: faint
Peroneal Artery RIGHT: 3 LEFT: 2-3

Comments:
RIGHT: Doppler ankle signals and ankle-arm index are normal-- no evidence of arterial occlusive disease of
the right lower extremity.
LEFT: Doppler ankle signals are minimally dampened with an abnormal ankle-arm index suggesting mild
arterial occlusive disease of the left lower extremity.

This is considered a Preliminary Report until physician interpretation and signature are added.
UCLA Vascular Laboratory is fully accredited by the Intersocietal Commission for the Accreditation of
Vascular Laboratories (ICAVL).

Eugene Hernandez, RVT (PLL#ECH)
Electronically signed (5/12/2005 11.4.20)

Dictated: 5/12/2005 10:58:32
  By: Eugene Hernandez, RVT (PLL#ECH)
  Reference number: FreeForm
Transcribed: 5/12/2005 10:58:32
  By: LL#ECH
  Reference number:
Received: 5/12/2005 10:59:32
Document ID Number: 3150656
Patient UI Number: 103232253
Filing number: 003

https://cds01.mednet.ucla.edu:447/esig/getDocHTML.asp?docNum=2952592&pdID=1011...   5/12/2005

Figure 21 Ankle Brachial test of May 12, 2005 showing left leg
is now .82 index, with no medical intervention!

MINK **RADIOLOGIC IMAGING**

8670 Wilshire Blvd
Ste 101
Beverly Hills, CA 90211
Phone: 310-358-2100
Fax: 310-358-2101

To: John Regan, M.D.
120 S. Spalding Dr.
Ste 400
Los Angeles, CA 90048
Fax: 310-385-8040

Name: **William Beeson**
MRN #: 033535
Phone: 714-256-2136
Exam Start: 1/18/06 2:43 pm
Referring Phys.: John Regan, M.D.

Exam: CT Angio pelvis with and without contrast
CPT Code(s): 72191 - CT ANGIOGRAPHY, PELVIS, W/O CONTRAST MATL(S), FOLLOWED BY CONTRAST MATL(S), W/IMAGE POST-PROCESSING

CT ANGIOGRAM OF THE PELVIS WITHOUT AND WITH INTRAVENOUS CONTRAST MATERIAL AND WITH REFORMATIONS:

Impression:
1) **Visualization of portions of the left common iliac artery is precluded by metallic streak artifact from the adjacent disk prosthesis at L3-4 and L4-5. Nevertheless, there are portions of the left common iliac artery that are visualized with evidence of marked stenosis that is probably greater than 90%. The left external and internal iliac arteries are normal as are the left common femoral, superficial femoral, and deep femoral. It is unlikely that complete occlusion of the left common iliac artery is present as there are no collaterals visualized in the left side of the pelvis or the thigh. It is recommended that these findings be confirmed with catheter angiography.**

Indications:
Patient had back surgery in October of 2004 with history of localized occlusion of the left common iliac artery adjacent to the vertebral body involved with surgery. There have been subsequent noninvasive arterial and duplex studies that have shown normal flow in the left lower extremity by the patient's history. The patient has a history of rest and exercise claudication of the left lower extremity. This is therefore requested for additional evaluation.

Technique:
Axial images were obtained from the level of the infrarenal abdominal aorta caudally to the level of the mid to distal thigh prior to intravenous contrast, using Toshiba Asteion Multidetector Helical CT with 3 mm thickness and 3 mm reconstruction. Nonionic iodinated contrast, 100 cc of Isovue 300, were then injected intravenously. Post contrast images through similar levels were obtained at 30 seconds and then at 60 seconds with 3 mm thickness and 2 mm reconstruction. These axial images were then transferred to the Vitrea workstation for maximum intensity projection and multiplanar reformation evaluation. The precontrast images are unavailable for review because of technical reasons. The two postcontrast series are available.

Findings:
There is extensive metallic streak artifact from the intervertebral disks at L3-4 and L4-5 and this precludes visualization of certain portions of the study. The infrarenal abdominal aorta is normal in size. The distal portion is not visualized at the L3-4 disk space. At the level of L4, the very proximal left common iliac artery is visualized and it is diminished in size measuring 4-5 mm. As it is observed passing laterally and caudally anterior to the L4 vertebral body, it becomes even further diminished in size measuring up to 2 mm with only very minimal contrast seen in the lumen. As it passes posterior to the inferior mesenteric artery, it measures approximately 1 mm.

Figure 22 CT Angio-scan, January 18th, 2006, page 1, note "no collaterals visualized in left side of the pelvis or thigh."

Beeson, William (Exam 65701)   MRN #: 033535

It is then not visualized anterior to the L4-5 disk space. Anterior to L5, it measures approximately 1 mm with very minimal intraluminal contrast. The very distal common iliac immediately proximal to the bifurcation is then well visualized measuring 6-7 mm in intraluminal dimension. The left external iliac and common femoral arteries are well visualized with contrast and appear normal. The superficial and deep femoral arteries on the left within the thigh enhance normally with contrast. The left internal iliac artery and its branching appear normal. No collateral vessels are seen in the left side of the pelvis or thigh.

There is a portion of the right common iliac artery that is not visualized because of the metallic streak artifact. The remainder that is seen is entirely normal. The right-sided arteries from the external iliac to the mid thigh are all well visualized and appear normal.

Incidentally noted is the presence of moderate to marked atrophy of the left rectus abdominis muscle. There is no evidence of lymphadenopathy in the pelvis or intraperitoneal fluid.

Marshall E. Bein M.D.

Marshall E. Bein
Electronically Signed: 1/19/06 8:22 am

Figure 23 CT Angio-scan, January 18th, 2006, page 2.

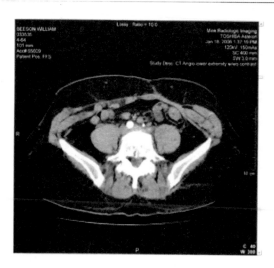

Figure 24 CT Angio x-ray taken January 18, 2006. Shows at 101 mm the view of the right iliac artery above vertebrae (large white circle to left area). Note the left iliac is not visible at 101 mm.

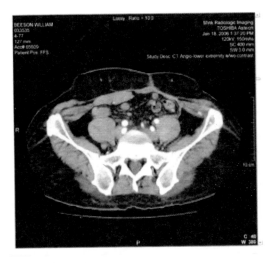

Figure 25 CT Angio x-ray taken January 18, 2006. Shows at 127 mm the view of the right femoral arteries above vertebrae (two white circles to left area). Note the left femoral arteries are now present (two white circle's to the right area) at 127 mm view. Report clearly states there are no collaterals present in the left side of the pelvic area. Nuclear dye would show up here if collaterals were present

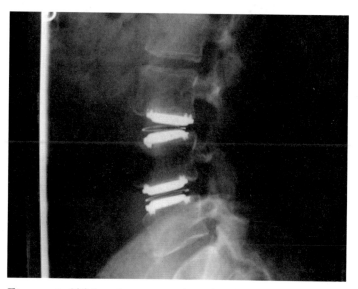

Figure 26 CT Lumbar x-ray taken January 18, 2006. Shows the position of the L3-L4 ADR implants are misplaced (post surgery #5). Top plate is too far posterior, with center core predisposed to dislodge toward anterior. Post-healing x-ray reveals anterior fusion, shadow area to left area in front of implant. Encapsulating the core.

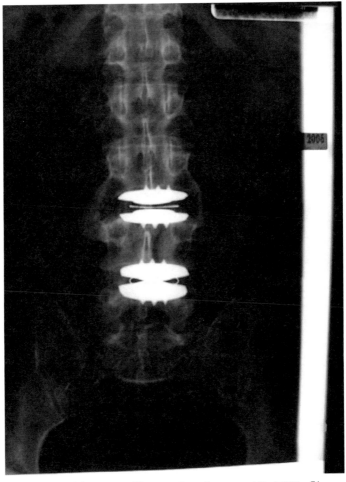

Figure 27 CT lumbar X-ray taken January 18, 2006. Shows the position of the L3-L4 implant. Photo taken post-healing; AP X-Rays reveals auto-fusion. Note the "halo" surrounding the implant.

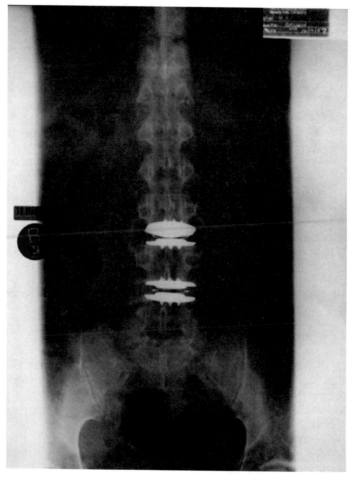

Figure 28 CT Lumbar x-ray taken May 18, 2005. Shows the position of the L3-L4 implant. Photo taken post-healing, AP x-ray reveals auto-fusion already formed! Three weeks post healing!

Figure 29 Picture of William Beeson taken mid-July 2005, at Pompey's Pillar, Wyoming.